It's another Quality Book from CGP

This book is for anyone doing Edexcel Modular GCSE Maths
at Intermediate Level.

It contains lots of tricky questions designed
to make you sweat — because that's the only
way you'll get any better.

It's also got some daft bits in to try and make
the whole experience at least vaguely
entertaining for you.

What CGP is all about

Our sole aim here at CGP is to produce the highest quality
books — carefully written, immaculately presented and
dangerously close to being funny.

Then we work our socks off to get them out to you
— at the cheapest possible prices.

Contents

Stage Three

Published by Coordination Group Publications Ltd.
Illustrated by Ruso Bradley, Lex Ward and Ashley Tyson

Coordinated by June Hall and Mark Haslam

Contributors:
Philip Wood
Margaret Carr
Barbara Coleman
John Lyons
Gordon Rutter
Claire Thompson

Updated by:
Philippa Falshaw
Tim Major
Julie Schofield

ISBN 1 84146 095 8

Groovy website: www.cgpbooks.co.uk

Printed by Elanders Hindson, Newcastle upon Tyne.
Clipart sources: CorelDRAW and VECTOR.

Questions on Negative Numbers

Negative numbers are pretty easy when you're used to them. Start by drawing yourself a number line, then count along it. After you've done a few questions, you'll find you can work them out in your head.

top tip

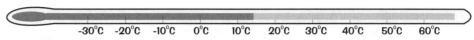

-30°C -20°C -10°C 0°C 10°C 20°C 30°C 40°C 50°C 60°C

(This first one's given you a thermometer, which has got its own number line, anyway.)

Q1   Work out the temperature <u>rise</u> for each of the following:
a) 10°C to 42°C   d) -4°C to 42°C   g) -30°C to -25°C
b) -10°C to 0°C   e) -29°C to 4°C   h) -18°C to 4°C
c) -20°C to 30°C   f) -19°C to -15°C   i) -15°C to 49°C

Q2   Work out the <u>drop</u> in temperature for each of the following:
a) 30°C to -10°C   d) 40°C to -30°C   g) 50°C to -30°C
b) 24°C to -4°C   e) -10°C to -25°C   h) -3°C to -5°C
c) 0°C to -17°C   f) -2°C to -27°C   i) -4°C to -29°C

Q3   Early one morning the temperature is <u>-3°C</u>. By noon it has risen <u>by 12°C</u>, falling again to <u>-5°C</u> by midnight.
a) What was the temperature at noon?
b) What was the difference in temperature between noon and midnight?
c) What was the difference in temperature between morning and midnight?

Q4   The temperature at mid-day was 18°C. By evening it had fallen by 23°C. What was the evening temperature?

Q5   What is the difference in height between the following points?
a) H and T   d) W and T
b) R and H   e) H and W
c) W and R   f) T and R

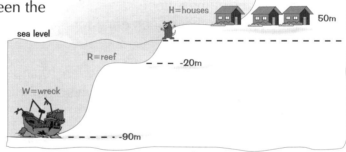

Hint: take the sea level as zero, then do a number line up the side.

Q6   A Roman soldier was born in 9 BC and died in the year AD 39. How long did he live?

Q7   A submarine is travelling at a depth of 500 m <u>below sea level</u> whilst directly overhead an aeroplane flies at 1300 m <u>above the sea</u>. How far apart are they?

Q8   Find the value of each of the following:
a) 13 – 5   e) -2 + 2   i) -3 + 0   m) -1 + 2 – -4
b) 6 – 7   f) -10 + 5   j) -3 – 4   n) 1 – -2 + 4
c) 10 – 20   g) -10 + 10   k) 5 – 10   o) -4 – -6 – 10
d) 4 – 11   h) -2 + 8   l) -20 – -100   p) 10 – -5 – 2

Q9   Work out the following:
a) -4 × -3   d) -8 ÷ 4   g) 2 × -2   j) 2 × -3 × -2
b) 5 × -2   e) -20 ÷ -10   h) -36 ÷ -12   k) -4 × -1 × -2
c) -12 ÷ -4   f) -4 × 4   i) -40 × 3   l) 10 ÷ (1 × -5)

Questions on Prime Numbers

 Basically, prime numbers don't divide by anything — and actually that's the best way to think of them. Have a go at the questions and you'll see what I mean.

---

1) <u>Prime Numbers</u> are all the numbers that <u>don't</u> come up in times tables.

2) The only way to get any <u>Prime Number</u> is 1 × ITSELF.

3) For example, the only numbers that multiply to give 5 are 1×5.

Q1 Use the digits **1, 2, 3, 7** alone or in pairs to make up:

    a) the smallest prime number

    b) a prime number greater than 20

    c) a prime number between 10 and 20

    d) two prime numbers whose sum is 20

    e) a number that is not prime.

> *Don't forget that 1 is not a prime — simple as that.*

1	②	③	4	⑤	6	7	8	9	10
11	12	13	14	15	16	17	18	19	20
21	22	23	24	25	26	27	28	29	30
31	32	33	34	35	36	37	38	39	40
41	42	43	44	45	46	47	48	49	50
51	52	53	54	55	56	57	58	59	60
61	62	63	64	65	66	67	68	69	70
71	72	73	74	75	76	77	78	79	80
81	82	83	84	85	86	87	88	89	90
91	92	93	94	95	96	97	98	99	100

Q2 Write down the first ten prime numbers.

Q3 Find all the prime numbers between 40 and 50.

Q4 In the <u>ten by ten square</u> opposite, ring all the prime numbers. (The first three have been done for you.)

Q5 Among the prime numbers between 10 and 100, find three which are still prime when their digits are reversed.

> *This stuff keeps coming up in the Exam — so make sure you can check if a number's prime or not. This is actually dead easy — have a look at the simple method on P.3 of The Revision Guide.*

Q6 What is the largest prime less than 500?

Q7 Give a reason for 27 not being a prime number.

Q8 How many prime numbers are even?

Q9 A school ran three evening classes: <u>judo, karate and kendo</u>. The judo class had 29 pupils, the karate class had 27 and the kendo class 23. For which classes did the teacher have difficulty dividing the pupils into equal groups?

Q10 Find three sets of three prime numbers which add up to the following numbers:

10   29   41

Questions on Multiples and Factors

This is real basic stuff — you just have to know your times tables. The only tricky bit is remembering which is a multiple and which is a factor — so learn the definitions and you won't go far wrong.

The **MULTIPLES** of a number are simply its **TIMES TABLE**	The **FACTORS** of a number are all the numbers that **DIVIDE INTO IT**.
e.g. The lowest three multiples of 3 are: <u>3</u> because 3 = 3 x 1 <u>6</u> because 6 = 3 x 2 <u>9</u> because 9 = 3 x 3	e.g. <u>12</u> can be made by: <u>1×12</u> or <u>2×6</u> or <u>3×4</u> so. the <u>factors of 12</u> are <u>1, 2, 3, 4, 6, 12</u>

Q1 From the numbers 1, 3, 4, 5, 6, 9, 10, 17, 23, 26, 27, 36 and 42, write down:
  a) all the <u>prime numbers</u>
  b) all the <u>multiples</u> of 6
  c) all the factors of 48.

Q2 List <u>all</u> the factors of the following numbers: 63, 80, 120, 220

Q3 Express each of the following as the sum of <u>two prime numbers</u>: 10, 20, 30

Q4 Sally is tiling a wall. The wall is 520 cm long and 300 cm high.
  a) Without wastage, what is the <u>largest</u> size square tile she can use?
  b) Tiles come in packs of 20. What is the <u>minimum</u> number of packs that Sally needs to buy?
  c) If Sally buys the minimum number of packs, how many tiles will <u>not</u> be used?

Q5 List all the factors for each of the following numbers
  a) 1   **c)** 15   **e)** 12   **g)** 23
  b) 3   **d)** 20   **f)** 33   **h)** 49

Q6 Write down the <u>ten lowest multiples</u> for each of the following numbers
  a) 18   **c)** 4   **e)** 10   **g)** 15
  b) 3   **d)** 7   **f)** 11   **h)** 20

Q7 Which of the following: 1, 2, 3, 4, 7, 8, 9, 12, 15, 23, 24, 36
  a) are multiples of 3?
  b) are prime numbers?

Basically, prime factors are just factors which are prime numbers — nice and easy, this bit.

Q8 Express the following as a <u>product of prime factors</u>:
  a) 7   **c)** 47   **e)** 648   **g)** 405
  b) 9   **d)** 105   **f)** 210   **h)** 25920

Q9 **a)** Write 1575 as a product of its <u>prime factors</u>.
  b) If $315 = 3^x \times 5^y \times 7^z$, find x, y and z.

The thing to remember is to always multiply out your answer — if you don't get back to the number you started with you've definitely missed a factor, so try again.

Q10 The prime factorisation of a certain number is $2^3 \times 7 \times 13$.
  a) What is the number?
  b) What is the prime factorisation of 1/2 of this number?
  c) What is the prime factorisation of 1/4 of this number?
  d) What is the prime factorisation of 1/8 of this number?

Questions on Multiples and Factors

Q11 From the numbers 1, 3, 6, 9 and 12, write down:
  a) a multiple of 4
  b) a prime number
  c) two <u>square</u> numbers
  d) three factors of 27.

Q12 Which of these numbers are not prime? Show a factor for evidence.
221, 35, 784, 20, 97

Q13 Gary can pay his bill either in all £2 coins or all £5 notes. What is the smallest amount that the bill can be?

Q14 George bought 3 identical lengths of ribbon. He cut the first into an exact number of 2 cm lengths, the second into an exact number of 12 cm lengths and the third into an exact number of 15 cm lengths.
What is the <u>smallest length</u> that the ribbons could have been?

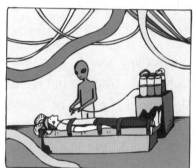

Q15 From the numbers
4, 9, 11, 20, 21, 26, 35, 44, 56, 65, 74, 83
find:
  a) <u>any square</u> numbers
  b) <u>all</u> the primes
  c) <u>all</u> the multiples of 4.

Q16 a) List the numbers between 5 and 35 inclusive which are <u>factors of 64</u>.
  b) List the numbers between 5 and 35 which are <u>multiples of 8</u>.
  c) Write down the numbers from parts **a)** and **b)** which are <u>both</u> multiples of 8 and factors of 64.

Q17 A packing carton measures 36 cm by 42 cm by 48 cm. The carton is filled with <u>cube</u> shaped boxes of chocolates.
  a) How big can the boxes of chocolates be?
  b) How many boxes of chocolates will fit in the carton?

Q18 List the first five odd numbers.
  a) If added together, what is their total?
  b) Write down the prime factorisation of the answer to part **a)**.

Q19 In the set of numbers from 10 to 40 write down:
  a) Any square numbers
  b) All the prime numbers
  c) A factor of 52
  d) A number divisible by 17.

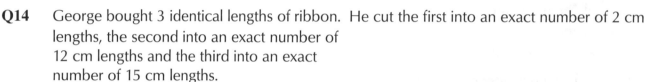

Hmmm, some of these don't tell you but they're still looking for factors and multiples. You really need to recognise them so practise them as often as it takes — not just once.

Questions on LCM and HCF

These two fancy names always put people off — but really they're dead easy. Just learn these simple facts:

> **1)** **The Lowest Common Multiple (LCM) is the <u>SMALLEST</u> number that will <u>DIVIDE BY ALL</u> the numbers in question.**

e.g.   3, 6, 9, 12, 15 are all multiples of 3
       5, 10, 15, 20, 25 are all multiples of 5
       The lowest number that is in both lists is 15, so 15 is the LCM of 3 and 5.

> **2)** **The Highest Common Factor (HCF) is the <u>BIGGEST</u> number that will <u>DIVIDE INTO ALL</u> the numbers in question.**

e.g.   1, 2, 4, 8 are all factors of 8
       1, 2, 3, 4, 6, 12 are all factors of 12
       The highest number that is in both lists is 4, so 4 is the HCF of 8 and 12.

Q1 **a)** List the <u>first ten</u> multiples of 6, <u>starting at 6</u>.
    b) List the <u>first ten</u> multiples of 5, <u>starting at 5</u>.
    c) What is the <u>LCM</u> of 5 and 6?

I tell you what, it's a lot easier to find the LCM or HCF once you've listed the factors or multiples. If you miss out this step it'll all go horribly wrong, believe me.

Q2 **a)** List all the factors of 30.
    b) List all the factors of 48.
    c) What is the <u>HCF</u> of 30 and 48?

Q3   For each set of numbers find the HCF.

a) 3, 5	**c)** 10, 15	**e)** 14, 21	**g)** 52, 72
b) 6, 8	**d)** 27, 48	**f)** 16, 32	**h)** 11, 33, 121

Q4   For each set of numbers, find the LCM.

a) 3, 5	**c)** 10, 15	**e)** 14, 21	**g)** 6, 15
b) 6, 8	**d)** 15, 18	**f)** 16, 32	**h)** 11, 33, 44

Q5   Lars, Rita and Alan regularly go swimming. Lars goes every 2 days, Rita goes every 3 days and Alan goes every 5 days. They <u>all</u> went swimming together on Friday 1st June.

    a) On what <u>date</u> will Lars and Rita next go swimming together?
    b) On what <u>date</u> will Rita and Alan next go swimming together?
    c) On what <u>day of the week</u> will all 3 next go swimming together?
    d) Which of the 3 (if any) will go swimming on 15th June?

Q6   For each set of numbers find the HCF.

a) 40, 60	**d)** 15, 45	**g)** 32, 64
b) 10, 40, 60	**e)** 15, 30, 45	**h)** 32, 48, 64
c) 10, 24, 40, 60	**f)** 15, 20, 30, 45	**i)** 16, 32, 48, 64

Q7   For each set of numbers find the LCM.

a) 40, 60	**d)** 15, 45	**g)** 32, 64
b) 10, 40, 60	**e)** 15, 30, 45	**h)** 32, 48, 64
c) 10, 24, 40, 60	**f)** 15, 20, 30, 45	**i)** 16, 32, 48, 64

Questions on Special Number Sequences

There are five special sequences: EVEN, ODD, SQUARE, CUBE and TRIANGLE NUMBERS. You really need to know them and their n^{th} terms.

 EVEN SQUARE ODD CUBE  TRIANGLE

Q1 What are these sequences called, and what are their next 3 terms?
a) 2, 4, 6, 8, ...
b) 1, 3, 5, 7, ...
c) 1, 4, 9, 16, ...
d) 1, 8, 27, 64, ...
e) 1, 3, 6, 10, ...

Q2 The following sequences are described in words. Write down their first four terms.
a) The prime numbers starting from 37.
b) The powers of 2 starting from 32.
c) The squares of odd numbers starting from $7^2 = 49$.
d) The triangular numbers starting from 15.
e) The powers of 10 starting from 1000.

Q3 Find the nth term of the following sequences:
a) 2, 4, 6, 8, ...
b) 1, 3, 5, 7, ...
c) 1, 4, 9, 16, ...
d) 4, 8, 16, 32, ...
e) 1, 8, 27, 64, ...
f) 1, 3, 6, 10, ...

Q4

Sequence A	1, 4, 9, 16, 25,...
Sequence B	3, 6, 9, 12, 15,...

a) Write down the next three terms in sequence A.
b) Write down the next three terms in sequence B.
c) Write down the nth term of sequence A.
d) Write down the nth term of sequence B.

Q5 The first four terms of a sequence are x, 4x, 9x, 16x.
a) For x = 2 write down the next two terms in the sequence.
b) For x = 2 write down the nth term in the sequence.
c) For x = 3 write down the nth term in the sequence.
d) Write down the nth term, valid for any value of x.
e) For x = ½ calculate the 75th term in the sequence.

Questions on Square and Cube Roots

"Square Root" means "What Number Times by Itself gives..."

E.g. The square roots of 64 are 8 and –8, the square roots of 36 are 6 and –6 etc.

That's because 8 × 8 = 64 and (–8) × (–8) = 64... OK, I was just checking.

Q1 Write down both answers for each of the following:
- a) $\sqrt{4}$
- b) $\sqrt{16}$
- c) $\sqrt{9}$
- d) $\sqrt{49}$
- e) $\sqrt{25}$
- f) $\sqrt{100}$
- g) $\sqrt{144}$
- h) $\sqrt{64}$
- i) $\sqrt{81}$

Q2 Use the $\sqrt{}$ button on your calculator to find the following positive square roots to the nearest whole number.
- a) $\sqrt{60}$
- b) $\sqrt{19}$
- c) $\sqrt{34}$
- d) $\sqrt{200}$
- e) $\sqrt{520}$
- f) $\sqrt{75}$
- g) $\sqrt{750}$
- h) $\sqrt{0.9}$
- i) $\sqrt{170}$
- j) $\sqrt{7220}$
- k) $\sqrt{1000050}$
- l) $\sqrt{27}$

Q3 Use your calculator to find, to 1d.p., the following square roots (two answers for each):
- a) $45^{1/2}$ b) $18^{1/2}$ c) $90^{1/2}$

Remember, the power ½ means a square root.

Q4 A square rug has an area of 235.3156 m². What is the <u>length</u> of an edge?

Q5 A square bowling green has an area of 2025 m². What is the <u>perimeter</u> of the green?

"Cube Root" means "What Number Times by Itself Twice gives..."

E.g. The cube root of 64 is 4, the cube root of 27 is 3 etc.

4 × 4 × 4 = 64, 3 × 3 × 3 = 27 — you get the picture...

Q6 Use your <u>calculator</u> to find the following:
- a) $\sqrt[3]{125}$
- b) $\sqrt[3]{1728}$
- c) $\sqrt[3]{1000}$
- d) $\sqrt[3]{729}$
- e) $\sqrt[3]{1331}$
- f) $\sqrt[3]{8000}$
- g) $\sqrt[3]{1}$
- h) $\sqrt[3]{0.125}$
- i) $\sqrt[3]{216}$
- j) $\sqrt[3]{343}$
- k) $\sqrt[3]{4096}$
- l) $\sqrt[3]{1000000}$

Questions on Fractions and Decimals

Remember, decimals are just a simple way of writing fractions — so it's easy to convert between the two. It's even easier if you get your calculator to do the hard work — so use it.

To convert _decimals to fractions,_ write the number as a fraction of 10, 100 etc, then cancel down.	To convert _fractions to decimals_ just use your calculator and divide.
Eg: $0.6 = \dfrac{6}{10} = \dfrac{3}{5}$ $0.15 = \dfrac{15}{100} = \dfrac{3}{20}$ $0.025 = \dfrac{25}{1000} = \dfrac{1}{40}$	Eg: $\dfrac{2}{3} = 2 \div 3 = 0.667$ $\dfrac{75}{100} = 75 \div 100 = 0.75$ $\dfrac{120}{150} = 120 \div 150 = 0.8$

Q1 Write the following fractions as decimals, giving your answer to 4 d.p.

a) $\dfrac{1}{2}$　　　e) $\dfrac{1}{16}$　　　i) $\dfrac{6}{7}$　　　m) $\dfrac{42}{51}$

b) $\dfrac{1}{4}$　　　f) $\dfrac{1}{25}$　　　j) $\dfrac{8}{15}$　　　n) $\dfrac{17}{19}$

c) $\dfrac{1}{10}$　　　g) $\dfrac{3}{4}$　　　k) $\dfrac{4}{21}$　　　o) $\dfrac{1}{11}$

d) $\dfrac{1}{20}$　　　h) $\dfrac{19}{20}$　　　l) $\dfrac{7}{18}$　　　p) $\dfrac{0}{100}$

Q2 Write the following decimals as fractions:

a) 0.1　　　e) 0.19　　　i) 0.25　　　m) 0.125

b) 0.2　　　f) 0.473　　　j) 0.3　　　n) 0.72

c) 0.34　　　g) 0.101　　　k) 0.4　　　o) 0.8764

d) 0.9　　　h) 0.16　　　l) 0.86　　　p) 1.2

Sometimes they put in extra details to confuse you. Just ignore it — simply write down the fraction or decimal then carry out the conversion. Go on, outsmart them.

Q3 During the football season, Chris collected 0.45 of his favourite team's stickers. Write this decimal as a fraction.

Q4 In the following conversion table fill in the gaps:

Q5 Over the course of a formula one motor race, 8/22 of the cars did not finish. Write this fraction as a decimal.

FRACTION	DECIMAL
$\frac{1}{10}$	
	0.15
	0.9
$\frac{1}{8}$	
$\frac{3}{16}$	
	0.375
$\frac{9}{20}$	
	0.625
$\frac{9}{8}$	

Questions on Decimals and Percentages

I reckon that converting decimals to percentages is about as easy as it gets — so make the most of it.

All you're doing is multiplying by 100 — it really couldn't be easier.

DECIMALS TO PERCENTAGES	Eg	0.5 = 50%
Move the <u>decimal point</u> <u>2 places</u> to the <u>right</u>.		0.62 = 62%
		0.359 = 35.9%

Q1 Express each of the following as a percentage:

a) 0.25   e) 1.0   i) 0.221   m) 0.4152
b) 0.5   f) 0.2   j) 0.546   n) 0.8406
c) 0.75   g) 0.11   k) 0.227   o) 0.3962
d) 0.1   h) 0.51   l) 0.713   p) 0.2828

PERCENTAGES TO DECIMALS	Eg	20% = 0.2
Move the <u>decimal point</u> <u>2 places</u> to the <u>left</u>.		75% = 0.75
		33.3% = 0.333

Now you're dividing by 100 — so just move the decimal point the other way. It's as simple as that.

Q2 Express each percentage as a decimal:

a) 50%   e) 62%   i) 60.2%   m) 75.16%
b) 12%   f) 17%   j) 54.9%   n) 44.02%
c) 40%   g) 16%   k) 43.1%   o) 98.25%
d) 34%   h) 77%   l) 78.8%   p) 82.65%

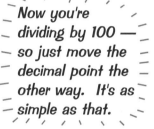

Q3 Harold estimates that 0.24 of his collection of racing snails are from Great Britain and Northern Ireland. Write this decimal as a percentage.

Q4 In the following conversion table fill in the gaps:

Q5 Jane reads in a newspaper that 34% of the population regularly watch soap operas on TV. Write this percentage as a decimal.

DECIMAL	PERCENTAGE
0.15	
	72%
0.6	
	18%
0.78	
	0.9%
0.33	
0.295	
	11.2%
	110%

Questions on Fractions and Percentages

For these, you'll need to use a combination of the methods on the last couple of pages.

Express 1/5 as a percentage	Express 60% as a fraction
1) Fraction to Decimal: $1 \div 5 = 0.2$ 2) Decimal to Percentage: (move the decimal point) <u>20%</u>	1) Percentage to Decimal: (move the decimal point) 0.6 2) Decimal to Fraction: $6/10 = 3/5$

Q1 Express each percentage as a fraction in its lowest terms:
- **a)** 25%
- **b)** 60%
- **c)** 45%
- **d)** 30%
- **e)** 51%
- **f)** 20%
- **g)** 76%
- **h)** 94%
- **i)** 98%
- **j)** 8%
- **k)** 65%
- **l)** 90%
- **m)** 8.2%
- **n)** 49.6%
- **o)** 88.6%
- **p)** 32.4%

Q2 Express each of the following as a percentage:

- **a)** $\dfrac{1}{2}$
- **b)** $\dfrac{1}{4}$
- **c)** $\dfrac{1}{8}$
- **d)** $\dfrac{3}{4}$

- **e)** $\dfrac{1}{25}$
- **f)** $\dfrac{2}{3}$
- **g)** $\dfrac{4}{15}$
- **h)** $\dfrac{2}{7}$

- **i)** $\dfrac{33}{100}$
- **j)** $\dfrac{9}{23}$
- **k)** $\dfrac{6}{7}$
- **l)** $\dfrac{3}{8}$

- **m)** $\dfrac{1}{13}$
- **n)** $\dfrac{2}{5}$
- **o)** $\dfrac{3}{7}$
- **p)** $\dfrac{2}{21}$

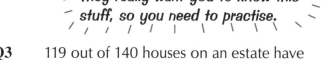

Yet more fractions and percentages. They really want you to know this stuff, so you need to practise.

Q3 119 out of 140 houses on an estate have video recorders. What percentage is this?

Q4 In a general knowledge quiz Tina scored 13/20. What percentage is this?

Q5 In the following conversion table fill in the gaps:

Q6 In a Physics exam, Tony scored 78/120. What percentage is this?

Bye!

Q7 In a survey 46/72 people said they had been on holiday to Spain. What percentage is this?

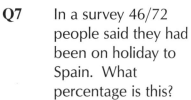

FRACTION	PERCENTAGE
	25%
	30%
$^7/_{10}$	
	33 $^1/_3$%
$^1/_4$	
$^5/_8$	
$^3/_8$	
	82%
	43.5%

Questions on Fractions without a Calculator

*I know doing fractions by hand is pretty scary stuff —
so you'd better learn those 4 Manual Methods.*

1) Multiplying	Multiply top and bottom separately: $\frac{2}{5} \times \frac{3}{7} = \frac{2 \times 3}{5 \times 7} = \frac{6}{35}$
2) Dividing	Turn the <u>2nd fraction UPSIDE DOWN</u> and then <u>multiply</u>: $\frac{2}{5} \div \frac{3}{7} = \frac{2}{5} \times \frac{7}{3} = \frac{2 \times 7}{5 \times 3} = \frac{14}{15}$
3) Adding, Subtracting	Add or subtract TOP LINES ONLY, but only once the bottom numbers are the same: $\frac{3}{5} + \frac{1}{5} = \frac{3+1}{5}, \frac{3}{5} - \frac{1}{5} = \frac{2}{5}$
4) Cancelling Down	<u>Divide top and bottom by the same number</u> 'till they won't go any further: $\frac{24}{32} = \frac{24 \div 8}{32 \div 8} = \frac{3}{4}$

Q1   Giving your answer as a fraction in its <u>lowest terms</u>, what fraction of each shape is shaded?

a)

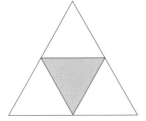

b)

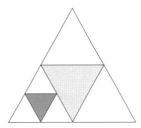

c)

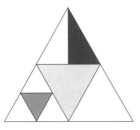

d)

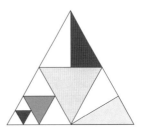

Q2   Cancel these fractions to their lowest terms:

a) $\frac{7}{21}$ c) $\frac{3}{5}$ e) $\frac{25}{100}$

b) $\frac{30}{90}$ d) $\frac{7}{35}$ f) $\frac{11}{121}$

Once you've ploughed your way through this little lot, you'll find they're not all that bad.

Q3   Express these as <u>mixed numbers</u> in their lowest terms:

a) $\frac{24}{8}$ c) $\frac{22}{10}$ e) $\frac{6}{3}$

b) $\frac{35}{6}$ d) $\frac{3}{2}$ f) $\frac{7}{4}$

no calculators!!

Q4   Express these as <u>top-heavy</u> fractions:

a) $1\frac{2}{3}$ c) $3\frac{1}{4}$ e) $2\frac{2}{5}$

b) $10\frac{1}{2}$ d) $1\frac{8}{9}$ f) $7\frac{3}{10}$

Questions on Fractions without a Calculator

Yeah, I agree — this is pretty tedious stuff but it looks like we're stuck with it. And you can make life a whole lot easier if you make the bottom numbers all the same for Q's 5 and 6.

Tip

Q5   Arrange the following in <u>ascending</u> order:

$$\frac{3}{6} \quad \frac{6}{3} \quad 3\frac{1}{6} \quad 6\frac{1}{3} \quad \frac{36}{3} \quad \frac{63}{6}$$

Q6   Write the following in <u>descending</u> order:

$$\frac{2}{5} \quad 2\frac{1}{5} \quad 2\frac{1}{3} \quad \frac{3}{4} \quad \frac{15}{10} \quad 1\frac{1}{2}$$

Q7   By giving each pair a <u>common denominator</u>, fill in <, > or = as appropriate:

a) $\frac{4}{5}$ and $\frac{3}{4}$ b) $\frac{3}{7}$ and $\frac{2}{9}$ c) $\frac{3}{6}$ and $\frac{1}{3}$ d) $\frac{4}{10}$ and $\frac{8}{20}$ e) $\frac{1}{12}$ and $\frac{3}{24}$

Don't forget to make the bottom numbers the same when adding (or subtracting) fractions as well. It's all a bit of a breeze, really.

Q8   Write down these fractions as decimals:

a) $\frac{3}{10}$ b) $\frac{1}{6}$ c) $\frac{2}{5}$ d) $\frac{2}{9}$ e) $\frac{3}{4}$ f) $\frac{7}{8}$

Q9   Write down these decimals as fractions in their lowest terms:

a) 0.7   b) 0.4   c) 0.32   d) 0.41   e) 0.95   f) 2.76

Q10   Without working them out, say whether each fraction has a terminating or recurring decimal:

a) $\frac{7}{10}$ b) $\frac{3}{4}$ c) $\frac{5}{7}$ d) $\frac{3}{17}$ e) $\frac{1}{40}$ f) $\frac{3}{8}$

Q11   Add the two fractions, giving your answer as a fraction in its lowest terms:

a) $\frac{7}{8}+\frac{3}{8}$ b) $\frac{1}{12}+\frac{3}{4}$ c) $1\frac{2}{5}+2\frac{2}{3}$ d) $\frac{1}{6}+4\frac{1}{3}$ e) $1\frac{3}{10}+\frac{2}{5}$

Q12   Evaluate, giving your answer as a fraction in its lowest terms:

a) $3\frac{1}{2}-\frac{2}{3}$ b) $10-\frac{2}{5}$ c) $1\frac{3}{4}-1\frac{1}{5}$ d) $4\frac{2}{3}-\frac{7}{9}$ e) $8-\frac{1}{8}$

Q13   Do the following multiplications, expressing the answers as fractions in their lowest terms:

a) $\frac{4}{3}\times\frac{3}{4}$ b) $2\frac{1}{6}\times3\frac{1}{3}$ c) $\frac{2}{5}\times\frac{3}{4}$ d) $2\frac{1}{2}\times\frac{3}{5}$ e) $10\frac{2}{7}\times\frac{7}{9}$

Q14   Carry out the following divisions, and express each answer in its lowest terms:

a) $\frac{1}{4}\div\frac{3}{8}$ b) $1\frac{1}{2}\div\frac{5}{12}$ c) $\frac{1}{9}\div\frac{2}{3}$ d) $10\frac{4}{5}\div\frac{9}{10}$ e) $3\frac{7}{11}\div1\frac{4}{11}$

Q15   Simplify the following:

a) $\dfrac{\left(\frac{1}{7}\times\frac{7}{8}\right)}{\frac{1}{8}}$ b) $\dfrac{\left(3\frac{1}{12}\div\frac{1}{6}\right)}{\left(1\frac{1}{5}\times\frac{5}{12}\right)}$ c) $\dfrac{\left(2\frac{2}{3}\right)}{\left(4\frac{1}{2}\times\frac{4}{3}\right)}$

Questions on Fractions with a Calculator

Don't get put off by all the padding in the questions — you've just got to pick out the important stuff. (And, don't forget to answer the right question — it sounds pretty dumb, but it's frightening how many people don't do it.)

Q1 At a college, two fifths of students are female, and three sevenths of these are part-time.
If there are 2100 students altogether, how many:

a) are <u>female</u> students?

b) are <u>part-time</u> female students?
If there are 1400 students altogether,

c) how many are <u>full-time female</u> students?

Don't forget to cancel your answer to its lowest terms. Just press the ▭ button — yeah, it really is that easy.

Q2 After a school fundraising event, a quarter of the money raised was spent on CD ROMs for the Learning Resource Centre and two thirds was spent on books. The remaining money, all <u>£49.47</u> of it, was paid into the bank. How much money was raised at the fundraiser?

Q3 In the summer, three friends ran a car cleaning service. They divided up the profits at the end of the summer according to the <u>proportion of cars</u> each had cleaned. Ali had washed 200 cars, Brenda had washed 50 and Chay had washed 175. The profits were £1700. How much did each person get?

Q4 The wage bill at an office is £2400 in total. Fred gets one sixth, Greg gets a fifth of the remainder and Hillary gets what is left. How much money are each of them paid?

Q5 If I pay my gas bill within seven days, I can have a <u>reduction</u> of an eighth of the price. If my bill is £120, how much can I save?

Q6 Jody sold her drum kit for £360 when she decided to buy a stereo. She <u>lost a fifth</u> of her money, but then needed to save only the remaining <u>one tenth</u> of the stereo's price. How much was the drum kit originally, and how much was the stereo?

Phew, thank goodness, that's the last page on fractions — but make sure you did all the questions — it's all on the Syllabus.

Questions on Percentages

Take it from me, there are three distinct types of percentage question — and one is easier than the other two. Basically, if you can see the % symbol you're onto a winner. Try these questions and you'll see what I mean.

1) "OF" means "×".
2) "PER CENT" means "OUT OF 100".

Example: 30% of 150 would be translated as $\dfrac{30}{100} \times 150 = 45$.

Q1   Calculate

a) 50% of £25.00

b) 20% of £5.25

c) 5% of £3.60

d) 36% of 400 kg

e) 12% of 75 g

f) 7% of 50 g

g) 12% of 300 rabbits

h) 18% of 150 cars

i) 0.5% of 89 m.

Q2   Terry has earnt £56 by washing cars. Whilst shopping he spent <u>20%</u> of his earnings on a CD, <u>5%</u> on his lunch and paid the rest into the bank.

a) How much money did Terry spend on food?

b) How much money did the CD cost?

Q3   John bought a new PC. The tag in the shop said it cost <u>£890+VAT</u>.

If VAT is charged at 17½%, how much did he pay?

Finding "something %" of "something-else" is really quite simple — so you'd better be sure you know how.

Q4   The admission price at Wonder World is <u>£18 for adults</u>. A child's ticket costs <u>60%</u> of the adult price.

a) How much will it cost for one adult and 4 children to enter Wonder World?

b) How much will two adults and three children spend on entrance tickets?

Q5   A boat manufacturer reduces the price of its small rubber dinghy from £42.00 to £31.50 what is the <u>percentage reduction</u>?

Q6   During a rain storm a water butt increased its weight from 10.4 kg to 13.52 kg. What was the <u>percentage increase</u>?

Q7   Rockwood School's results for A-Level Biology are given in the table.

A-Level Biology Results					
Grade	A	B	C	D	E
Frequency	7	10	15	12	5

a) What percentage of candidates achieved grade A?

b) What percentage of candidates achieved grade A, B or C?

c) What percentage of candidates didn't achieve grade A, B or C?

Questions on Substituting Values

BODMAS — this funny little word helps you remember in which order to work formulas out. The example below shows you how to use it. Oh and by the way "**O**ther" might not seem important, but it means things like powers, square and cube roots, etc — so it is.

Brackets, **O**ther, **D**ivision, **M**ultiplication, **A**ddition, **S**ubtraction

Example: if $z = \frac{x}{10} + (y - 3)^2$ find the value of z when x = 40 and y = 13.

1) Write down the formula with the numbers substituted in,

$$z = \frac{40}{10} + (13 - 3)^2$$

2) **B**rackets first $\qquad z = \frac{40}{10} + (10)^2$

3) **O**ther next, so square $\qquad z = \frac{40}{10} + 100$

4) **D**ivision before **A**ddition $\qquad z = 4 + 100$

$$\underline{z = 104}$$

Q1 If x = 3 and y = 6 find the value of the following expressions:

a) x + 2y

b) 2x ÷ y

c) 4(x + y)

d) $(y - x)^2$

e) $2x^2$

f) $2y^2$

Q2 The cost of framing a picture, C pence, depends on the <u>dimensions of the picture</u>. If C = 10L + 5W, where L is the length in cm and W is the width in cm, then find the cost of framing:

a) a picture 40cm long by 24cm wide

b) a square picture of sides 30cm.

Q3 If V = lwh, find V when,

a) l = 7, w = 5, h = 2   b) l = 12, w = 8, h = 5.

Q4 Using the formula $z = (x - 10)^2$, find the value of z when,

a) x = 20

b) x = 15

c) x = -1

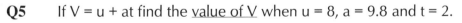

Use the memory button on your calc, so you don't have to keep typing things in yourself.

Q5 If V = u + at find the <u>value of V</u> when u = 8, a = 9.8 and t = 2.

Q6 If $V = \pi r^2 h$ find the value of V when r = 4 and h = 6. Take π = 3.14.

Q7 The cost, C pence, of hiring a taxi depends on the number, n, of miles you travel in it, where C = 100 + 25n. Find C when

a) n = 2

b) n = 10

c) n = 15

Q8 The time taken to cook a chicken is given as 20 minutes per lb plus 20 minutes extra. Find the time needed to cook a chicken weighing

a) 4 lb

b) 7.5 lb.

16

Questions on Substituting Values

I know some of the formulas on this page are easy ones, which I'm sure you can do without the aid of BODMAS — but use it anyway, 'cos it's all good practice.

Q9 The area of a triangle, A , is given by the formula:
A = ½ (base x height)
Find the area of the following triangles:-

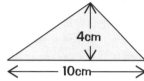 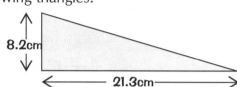 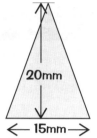

Q10 An estate agent is paid according to the formula £P = £950m +£100h where £P is the estate agent's pay for working m months and selling h houses.
a) How much does the estate agent <u>earn in 2 months</u> if he sells 1 house?
b) How much does the estate agent <u>earn in 5 months</u> if he sells 4 houses?
c) How much does the estate agent <u>earn per annum</u> if he sells on average one house per month?

Q11 The area of a circle A is given by the formula $A = \pi r^2$.
Taking $\pi = 3.14$, find the area of the circles a), b) and c):

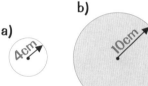 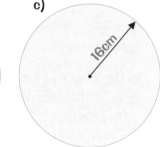

Q12 In a Physics experiment two resistors of strengths P and Q are connected in an electrical circuit and their total resistance R Ohms is given by $R = \frac{PQ}{P+Q}$.
Find the total resistance of the circuit when
a) P=3 and Q=3
b) P=60 and Q=40.

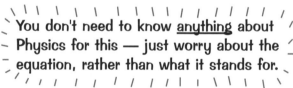
You don't need to know <u>anything</u> about Physics for this — just worry about the equation, rather than what it stands for.

Q13 The sum of the <u>interior angles</u>, S, of a polygon with n sides, is given by the formula S = 180(n–2). Find the value of S for the three polygons.

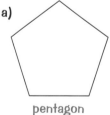 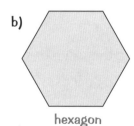 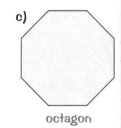

pentagon   hexagon   octagon

Q14 What is the value of
a) $3x^2$
b) $(x+y)^2$
c) $(x-y)/2$
d) $\sqrt{x} + \sqrt{y}$
e) $2(x^2-y^2)$
f) $2(x-y)^2$ when x=9 and y=4 ?

Q15 To change temperature from °F to °C you can use the formula $C = \frac{5}{9}(F-32)$.
Change the following temperatures to °C:
a) 95°F   b) 113°F   c) 167°F   d) 185°F   e) 14°F

Questions on Basic Algebra

 OK, it says basic, but it isn't a doddle. Things'll easily go wrong unless you really think about what you're doing — keep going 'till your brain hurts.

Simplifying means collecting **like terms** together:	**Expanding** means removing brackets:
$8x^2 + 2x + 4x^2 - x + 4$ becomes $12x^2 + x + 4$ x^2 term, x term, x^2 term, x term, number term	Eg $4(x+y) = 4x + 4y$ $x(2+x) = 2x + x^2$ $-(a+b) = -a - b$

Q1 By collecting like terms, simplify the following:

a) $3x + 4y + 12x - 5y$

b) $11a + 6b + 24a + 18b$

c) $9f + 16g - 15f - 30g$

d) $14ab + 12cd - ab + 2cd$

e) $4x^2 + 3x + 2x^2 - 5x$

f) $13x^2 - 9x - x^2 + 4x$

g) $3y^2 + 2y - 4 + 8y^2 - y + 10$

h) $5xy + 6x + 2xy + 12x$

i) $9abc + 10ab + 14abc$

j) $13xy + 7yx$

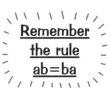 Remember the rule $ab = ba$

Q2 Simplify the following:

a) $x(x+1)$

b) $-2(4+x)$

c) $-(z+1)$

d) $x^2(2+y)$

e) $x^2(3x+4+y)$

f) $5(p^3+p)$

g) $15(2q+3r^2)$

h) $-4(e^2-f+4)$

i) $2p(p+q) - 3p(p+2q)$

j) $2x(4+x) + 3x(x-1)$

k) $x(2x+y) + 3y(3x+2y)$

l) $a(b+c) + b(a+c) + c(a+b)$

Q3 Simplify the following algebraic fractions by cancelling any common factors.

a) $\dfrac{xyz}{xy}$

b) $\dfrac{a(b-4)}{(b-4)}$

c) $\dfrac{4xy(z-3)(z+2)}{2x(z+2)}$

d) $\dfrac{9x^2y^2z(x-2)}{3xyz(x-2)}$

e) $\dfrac{3(a-4)^2(a-2)(a-1)}{9bc(a-1)(a-4)}$

f) $\dfrac{12x^2(a-4)^3(y-9)^4}{3x(a-4)^2(y-9)^2(z-2)}$

Q4 Remove the brackets and simplify:

a) $(x+1)(x+2)$

b) $(x+3)(x+2)$

c) $(x+4)(x+5)$

d) $(x+10)(x+2)$

e) $(x+5)(x-1)$

f) $(x+2)(x-3)$

g) $(x-3)(x+1)$

h) $(x-4)(x+5)$

i) $(x-2)(x-1)$

j) $(x-3)(x-4)$

k) $(x-2)(x-5)$

l) $(x-10)(x-3)$

m) $(x-5)(x+10)$

n) $(5+x)(2+x)$

o) $(x-2)(3+x)$

p) $(4-x)(8-x)$

Q5 For each large rectangle write down the area of the four <u>small</u> rectangles, and hence find an <u>expression</u> for the area of the <u>large</u> rectangle.

a)
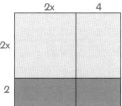

b)
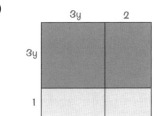

c)
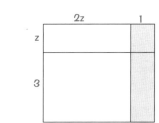

Questions on Basic Algebra

FACTORISING is just <u>putting the brackets back in</u>.
And when you've just spent all that time getting rid of them...

$$7x^2 + 21xy = 7x(x + 3y)$$

| largest number that will go into 7 and 21 | highest power of x, that will go into each term | y is not in every term so it is not a common factor, and goes inside the brackets |

Q6 Rewrite these expressions using brackets. Look for any <u>common factors</u>.

a) $2x + 4y$ e) $2x + 12$ i) $4x - 40$ m) $10x - 8y$

b) $3x + 12y$ f) $3x + 15$ j) $5x - 15$ n) $36x - 27y$

c) $9x + 3y$ g) $24 + 12x$ k) $7x - 49$ o) $24x - 32y$

d) $16x + 4y$ h) $30 + 10x$ l) $8x - 32$ p) $24x - 42$

Q7 Each expression below has <u>2x</u> as a common factor. Factorise the following:

a) $2xy + 4x^2$ c) $2xy - 16x^2z$ e) $10x^2 - 6x^2$ g) $2xy - 4xz$

b) $2xy - 8x^2$ d) $4xy - 6x^2$ f) $10x^2 - 6x$ h) $12xy + 10xz$

Q8 Each term below has <u>a²</u> as a common factor. Factorise the following:

a) $a^2b + a^2c$ d) $2a^2b + 3a^2c$ g) $2a^2x + 3a^2y + 4a^2z$

b) $4a^2 + 7a^2$ e) $10a^2b^2 + 9a^2c^2$ h) $2a^2b + 3a^2c + a^2$

c) $5a^2 + 13a^2b$ f) $a^3 + a^2y$ i) $a^2b^2 + a^2c^2$

Q9 Each term below has <u>4xyz</u> as a common factor. Factorise the following:

a) $4xyz + 8xyz$ c) $8xyz + 16x^2yz$

b) $8xyz + 12xyz$ d) $20x^2y^2z + 16xyz^2$

Q10 Factorise:

a) $7a^2bc^2 + 14ab^2c + 21ab^2c^2 + 28a^2b^2c^2$

b) $100x^2yz + 90x^3yz + 80x^2y^2z + 70x^2yz + 60x^2yz^2$

Q11 What is the difference between $2a^2 + 3b^2 + 4a - b + 11$ and $a^2 + b^2 + 3a - 2b + 3$?

Q12 A rectangular bar of chocolate consists of 20 small rectangular pieces as shown. The size of a small rectangular piece of chocolate is 2 cm by x cm.

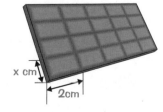

a) Write down an expression for the width of the whole bar.

b) Write down an expression for the perimeter of the whole bar.

c) Write down an expression for the area of the whole bar.

d) If I ate 6 small rectangular pieces of chocolate, what is the area of the remaining piece left over?

Questions on Solving Equations

OK, so you've noticed this page starts off all right, but things do get a bit hairy later on — so give yourself a head start by practising your algebra skills on the easy ones.

Q1   Solve the following:

a) 4x = 20

b) 7x = 28

c) x + 3 = 11

d) x + 19 = 23

e) x – 6 = 13

f) 7x = -14

g) 2x = -18

h) x + 5 = -3

i) x/2 = 22

j) x/7 = 3

k) x/5 = 8

l) 10x = 100

m) 2x + 1 = 7

n) 2x + 4 = 5

o) 7x + 5 = 54

p) 6x – 7 = 41

q) 2x + 7 = 13

r) 3x – 2 = 19

Q2   When eight is subtracted from a number the result is thirty-two.

a) Write this information as an equation.

b) Solve your equation to <u>find the number</u>.

Q3   When a number is multiplied by three and seven is added, the result is nineteen.

a) Write this information <u>as an equation</u>.

b) Solve your equation to find the number.

Q4   Andrew, Ben and Carl collect stamps. Andrew has 86 more than Ben and Carl has 156 more than Ben. If Ben has x stamps write down an expression for the number of stamps owned by:

a) Andrew

b) Carl

Altogether they have 776 stamps.

c) Using your <u>previous answers</u> write down and solve an equation in x.

d) How many stamps do Andrew and Carl have each?

Q5   Mary is y years old. Her father is 4 times older than Mary. Her mother is 7 years younger than her father. If their three ages add up to 101 years, find the value of y.
Find the ages of Mary's parents.

Q6   A girl spent t minutes on her Chemistry homework. She spent twice as long on her Maths homework and her English homework took her 15 minutes longer than her Chemistry did. If she spent a total of 95 minutes working, find the value of t.

Q7   Mr Smith sent his car to the local garage. He spent £x on new parts, four times this amount on labour and finally £29 for an MOT test. If the total bill was for £106.50, find the value of x.

Q8   Solve the following:

a) 3x – 4 = 2x + 4

b) 3x – 8 = 5x – 20

c) 23 – x = x + 11

d) 8x + 7 = 6x – 9

e) 4x + 7 = x – 2

f) 8x + 3 = 10x – 7

g) 3x – 2.5 = 5

h) 5x – 2 = ½x + 7

i) 2x – 5 = ½x + 4

j) 3x + 7 = ½x + 2

k) 3(x + 1) = 9

l) 2(x – 3) – (x – 2) = 5

m) 5(x + 2) – 3(x – 5) = 29

n) 2(x + 2) + 3(x + 4) = 31

Questions on Solving Equations

Well, the good thing about doing all of these is that soon you'll be able to do algebra with your eyes closed. That'll be nice.

Q9   Solve the following:
   a) $3(7 - 2x) = 2(5 - 4x)$
   b) $6(x + 2) + 4(x - 3) = 50$
   c) $2(4x - 12) = 6(3x - 4)$
   d) $2(2x - 1) = 3(4x + 2)$
   e) $5(x + 3) = 4(2x - 5)$
   f) $2(2x + 3) + 5(3x + 1) = 6(3x + 4)$
   g) $4(3x + 2) + 3 = 3(2x - 5) + 2$
   h) $10(x + 3) - 4(x - 2) = 7(x + 5)$
   i) $5(4x + 3) = 4(7x - 5) + 3(9 - 2x)$
   j) $3(7 + 2x) + 2(1 - x) = 19$

Q10   Find x in the following:
   a) $x/2 + 4 = 7$
   b) $8 + x/3 = 11$
   c) $20 + x/4 = 22$
   d) $x/3 + 7 = 12$
   e) $x/10 + 18 = 29$
   f) $5 - x/2 = 3$
   g) $10 - x/3 = 1$
   h) $50 - x/4 = 18$
   i) $17 - x/3 = 5$
   j) $41 - x/11 = 35$
   k) $2x/5 = 4$
   l) $3x/4 = 75$
   m) $2x/3 = 14$
   n) $x/100 = 5$
   o) $x/100 - 3 = 4$
   p) $40/x = 8$
   q) $55/x = 11$
   r) $200/x = 25$
   s) $120/x = 16$
   t) $90/x = 20$

Q11   In a darts competition, Susan scored 147 more than John and three times as much as Elizabeth. If their combined score came to 336, find their individual scores.

Q12   The sum of <u>two consecutive</u> numbers is 267.
   a) Write this information as an equation.
   b) Solve your equation to find the two numbers.

Q13   Solve the following:
   a) $8m - \frac{1}{2} = 6m + 7$
   b) $\frac{1}{2}p - 13 = 3p + 7$
   c) $\frac{3}{4}t + 6 = \frac{1}{4}t + 8$
   d) $\frac{1}{2}z + 2 = \frac{1}{4}z + 6$

> Get rid of any unwanted fractions by multiplying the <u>whole equation</u> by the bottom number. If you've got a couple of fractions with different numbers at the bottom, multiply by their LCM (see P.5).
>
> Don't forget to multiply <u>each</u> term by the <u>same thing</u> or things'll go a bit pear-shaped.

Q14   Solve the following:
   a) $18 - 3(7 - 2x) + 4x = 22$
   b) $6x = 2(x - 4)$
   c) $3x + 24 + 2(x - 3) = 28$
   d) $4x - 7 - 7(6 - x) = 14$

Q15   A piece of ribbon is 26 cm long. It is cut into two pieces, which differ by 6 cm. Let the length of the shorter piece be x cm, and form an equation in x. Find the <u>two lengths</u>.

Q16   Two men are decorating a room. One has painted 20 m² and the other has painted only 6 m². They continue painting and both manage to paint another x m² each. If the first man has painted exactly three times the area painted by the second man, find x.

Questions on Number Patterns

Number sequences are fun — they're often nothing more than pretty pictures.

Q1

a) Write down the number of dots in each square.
b) Give the number of dots for the next three squares in the sequence.
c) Write down a formula for the number of dots in the nth square of the sequence.

Q2   Using pencils, Tom made a pattern:

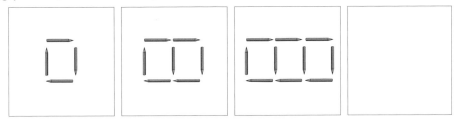

a) Write down the number of pencils in each group.
b) How many pencils would be in the next group along?
c) Find a formula for the number of pencils in the nth group.

Don't let the pictures confuse you, just write down a number for each picture and you're away.

Q3   Using matchsticks, Jessica made a simple diagram of a house:
If houses that are joined together still require their own roof,

a) how many matchsticks would she need to complete a pair of semi-detached houses?
b) how many matchsticks would she need to complete a set of three terraced houses?
c) how many matchsticks would she need to make four terraced houses?
d) what is the formula for n terraced houses?

Q4

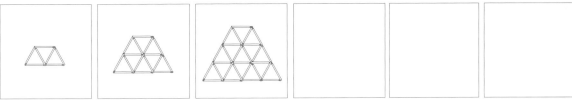

The pattern above is based on individual triangles.
a) Write down the number of small triangles in each group.
b) Work out the number of small triangles that would be in each of the next three groups.
c) Find a formula for the number of small triangles in the nth term of the pattern.

STAGE ONE

Questions on Number Patterns

Q5 A square tile pattern is formed with black and white tiles. In the centre there is always a black tile. The rest of the pattern is made up of alternating black and white tiles, with the four corner tiles of the square always being black.
The first term of the pattern is shown.
Work out the formula for:

a) the number of black tiles

b) the number of white tiles

c) the total number of tiles.

This is what you need to know to find the nth term of a "Common Difference Type" sequence:

Common Difference Type: nth term = dn + (a − d)
1) "a" is the <u>FIRST TERM</u> in the sequence.
2) "d" is the <u>COMMON DIFFERENCE.</u>

Q6 In the following sequences, write down the next 3 terms and the nth term:

a) 2, 5, 8, 11,...

b) 7, 12, 17, 22,...

c) 1, 11, 21, 31,...

d) 49, 56, 63, 70,...

Q7 Jeff is collecting the post for his grandmother while she is away on holiday. On the first day she was away she received 3 letters. On the second day the pile of letters had grown to 6. By the third day, Jeff had 9 letters in all. This pattern continued while his grandmother was away, and she returned from her holiday on the ninth day.

a) How many letters were waiting for her?

b) How many letters would have been waiting if she had returned on the nth day?

Changing Difference Type: nth term = a + (n - 1)d + ½(n - 1)(n - 2)C
1) "a" is the <u>first term</u> in the sequence,
2) "d" is the <u>first difference</u> and
3) "C" is the <u>change between one difference and the next</u>.

Q8 Write down the next three terms and nth term of:

a) 2, 5, 9, 14,...

b) 3, 6, 11, 18,...

c) 6, 9, 16, 27,...

d) 11, 16, 24, 35,...

Questions on Coordinates

It's easy to make a hash of this, but what you've got to remember is:
1) **X** comes before **Y**, and 2) **X** is a-cross (hmmm).

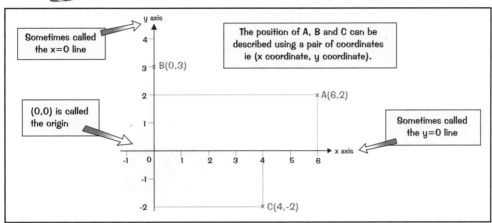

If you forget these, it'll all go completely pear-shaped.

Q1 ABCD is a <u>parallelogram</u>. A is (-1, 3), B is (-2,-1) and C is (4,-1).
Draw axes with x from -4 to 5 and y from -2 to 4.
Plot A, B and C then find the <u>missing coordinates</u> for D.

Q2 Draw axes with x from -9 to 9 and y from -12 to 12.
On the <u>same</u> set of axes draw the following shapes and find their <u>missing pair of coordinates</u>.

a) ABCD is a <u>square</u>
A is (1, 1)
B is ?
C is (-3,-3)
D is (-3, 1)

b) ABCD is a <u>parallelogram</u>
A is (2, 8)
B is (6, 8)
C is ?
D is (1, 5)

c) ABCD is a <u>rectangle</u>
A is ?
B is (3,-8)
C is (3,-6)
D is (-5,-6)

d) ABCD is a <u>kite</u>
A is (-9, 3)
B is (-6, 8)
C is (-4, 8)
D is ?

e) ABCD is a <u>parallelogram</u>
A is (-2,-10)
B is (4,-10)
C is (6,-12)
D is ?

f) ABCD is a <u>parallelogram</u>
A is (-8, 10)
B is (-6, 10)
C is ?
D is (-5, 12)

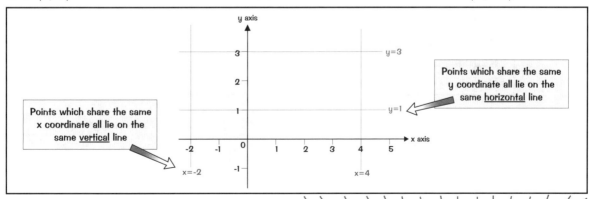

Q3 ABCD is a <u>rectangle</u> with the line <u>x = 0</u> as a <u>line of symmetry</u>.
Draw axes with x from -3 to 3 and y from -3 to 3.
If A = (-2,-2) and B is (-2, 1), find the <u>coordinates of C and D</u>.

I'm afraid you'll just have to get the hang of using things like "the line x = 4", as they seem to prefer it to "a vertical line through the point 4 on the horizontal axis". Yeah, that is a bit long winded, I guess — so maybe they've got a point...

Questions on Regular Polygons

The one thing they're <u>guaranteed</u> to ask you about is <u>Interior and Exterior Angles</u> — you'd better get learning those formulas...

Q1   Describe what a <u>regular</u> polygon is.

Q2   What sort of triangles occur in a <u>regular hexagon</u> when each vertex is joined to the centre by a straight line?

Q3   What sort of triangles occur in every regular polygon (<u>except</u> a hexagon), when each vertex is joined to the centre by a straight line?

Q4   What are the names given to the two types of angles associated with regular polygons?

Q5   What formula links interior with exterior angles?

Q6   What formula could be used to work out the <u>exterior</u> angle of a regular polygon if the number of sides of the regular polygon is known?

Q7   What formula could be used to work out the <u>interior</u> angle of a regular polygon if the number of sides of the regular polygon is known?

Q8   Complete the following table:

Name	Sides	Lines of Symmetry	Order of Rotational Symmetry
Equilateral Triangle			
Square		4	
Regular Pentagon			
Regular Hexagon	6		
Regular Heptagon	7		
Regular Octagon			8
Regular Decagon	10		

Q9   A square and a regular hexagon are placed adjacent to each other.
a) What is the <u>size</u> of ∠PQW?
b) What is the <u>size</u> of ∠PRW?
c) How many sides has the <u>regular polygon</u> that has ∠PQW as one of its angles?

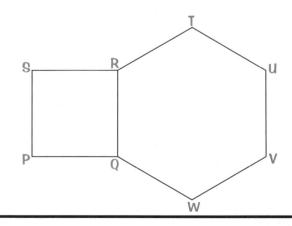

Questions on Regular Polygons

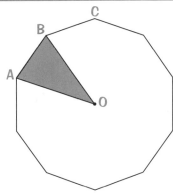

Q10   Here is a <u>regular decagon</u>.
Calculate:
a) $\angle AOB$
b) $\angle OBA$
c) $\angle ABC$

Q11   In a regular <u>7 sided</u> polygon, what is the size of one interior angle, is it
a) $128\frac{4}{7}°$ b) $135°$ c) $120°$ d) $112\frac{2}{7}°$ or   e) $140°$?

Q12   A regular polygon has an <u>interior</u> angle of $160°$. Calculate
a) the size of each exterior angle
b) how many sides it has.

Q13   The <u>exterior</u> angle of a <u>regular</u> polygon is $24°$. How many sides does it have?

Q14 a) Find the size of the interior angles of a <u>regular</u> 24 sided polygon.

  b) From this answer calculate one <u>exterior</u> angle and show that the <u>sum</u> of the exterior angles equals $360°$.

Q15   Complete the table, then write a sentence to describe what is happening to the values of the interior/exterior angles as the number of sides increases.

Number of sides	Name	Interior angle	Exterior angle
5			
6			
7	Heptagon		
8			
9	Nonagon	$140°$	
10		$144°$	
11	Hendecagon	$147.\ddot{2}72\ddot{7}°$	
12			
15			
18			
24			

Questions on Symmetry

They do say that bad things happen in threes... and now you've got to learn three types of symmetry — but don't worry, I reckon their names pretty much give the game away.

There are THREE types of symmetry:	
1) LINE SYMMETRY	You can draw a mirror line across the object and both sides will fold together exactly.
2) PLANE SYMMETRY	This applies to 3-D solids. You can draw a plane mirror surface through the solid to make the shape exactly the same on both sides of the plane.
3) ROTATIONAL SYMMETRY	You can rotate the shape or drawing into different positions that all look exactly the same.

Q1 Draw _all_ the lines of symmetry for each of the following shapes. (Some shapes may have no lines of symmetry)

a)　　　　b)　　　　c)　　　　d)　　　　e)　　　　f)

These questions are a piece of cake if you use tracing paper — and remember you can use it in the Exam, so take some with you or ask for it.

Q2 What is the <u>order of rotational symmetry</u> for each of the following shapes ?

a)　　　　　　b)　　　　　　c)　　　　　　d)

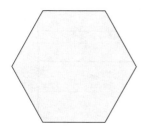
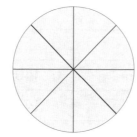
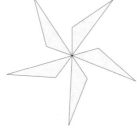
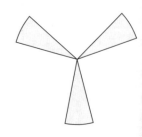

Q3 Mark in the <u>lines of symmetry</u> of the following letters. State the <u>order</u> of rotational symmetry for each one.

MHVBAKSZ

Questions on Symmetry

Q4 Draw an example of each of the following shapes. Put in the <u>axes of symmetry</u> and state the <u>order</u> of rotational symmetry.

a) An equilateral triangle.

b) An isosceles triangle.

c) A rhombus.

d) An isosceles trapesium.

e) A regular octagon.

f) A parallelogram.

Q5 On each cube draw in a different <u>plane of symmetry</u>.

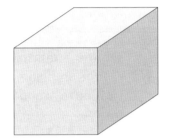 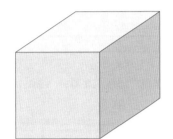 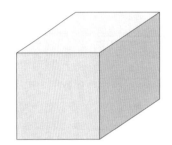

Q6 Here is a cuboid: Is the plane a plane of symmetry?

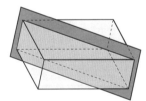

Q7 How many planes of symmetry does this <u>triangular prism</u> have?

Q8 How many planes of symmetry does a <u>circular cone</u> have?

Q9 In the square based pyramid shown, is this a plane of symmetry?

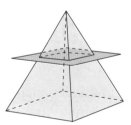

Q10 Draw in another plane of symmetry, which is <u>perpendicular</u> to the one drawn in the diagram.

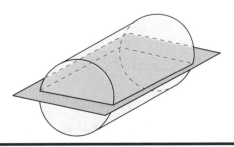

Questions on Transformations

You've got to be able to give all the details for each type — and it **will** be in the Exam.

Use the word **TERRY** to remember the 4 transformations :	Always specifiy **ALL** the details:
T ranslation	1) VECTOR OF TRANSLATION
E nlargement	1) SCALE FACTOR 2) CENTRE OF ENLARGEMENT
R eflection	1) MIRROR LINE
R otation	1) ANGLE TURNED 2) DIRECTION 3) CENTRE OF ROTATION
Y	

Q1 Write down the <u>translation vectors</u> for the translations shown.

The Y doesn't stand for anything, in case you're wondering...

a)

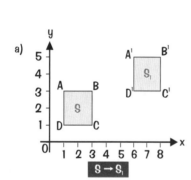

b)

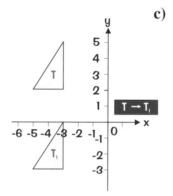

c)

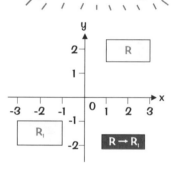

Q2

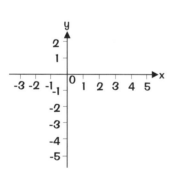

Using this set of axes, plot D (3,-2).

Now <u>translate</u> the point D, and <u>draw the image</u> of point D after translation under each of the vectors:

a) $\begin{pmatrix} 1 \\ 2 \end{pmatrix}$, Label D_1

c) $\begin{pmatrix} 1 \\ -1 \end{pmatrix}$, Label D_3

b) $\begin{pmatrix} -3 \\ -2 \end{pmatrix}$, Label D_2

d) $\begin{pmatrix} -4 \\ 0 \end{pmatrix}$, Label D_4

Q3 A translation maps (4, 2) onto (7, 4). What is the image point of (-1, 6) under the <u>identical translation?</u>

Q4 A translation maps the point P(2, 1) onto P_1(1, 2). P_1 is then mapped onto P_2 via the translation $\begin{pmatrix} -4 \\ 2 \end{pmatrix}$.

a) What is the translation that maps P onto P_1?
b) Where is the point P_2?
c) What <u>single translation</u> would map P onto P_2, directly?
d) What <u>single translation</u> would map P_2 back to P, directly?

Questions on Transformations

There are only 3 transformations covered in Stage One — Translation, Rotation and Reflection. Make sure you know them all — and I mean really know them — so you can spot them in combinations.

Q5 Draw the result of <u>reflecting</u> this shape in

a) the x-axis

b) the y-axis.

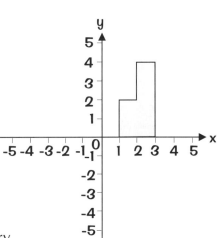

Q6 Plot each of the following points on graph paper. Join them together with straight lines in alphabetic order.

A(0,0) B(0, 2) C (2, 4)
D(4, 2) E(2,2) F(2,0)

a) Reflect the shape <u>in the y-axis</u>.

b) Reflect the original shape <u>in the x-axis</u>.

c) Complete the drawing so that it has <u>2 lines of symmetry</u>.

Q7 PQRS is a parallelogram where P is the point (-1, 3), Q is the point (-2, 1½), R is the point (?,?) and S is the point (-3, 3).

a) What are the coordinates of the point R?

b) Plot the parallelogram on squared paper.

c) Draw in the <u>line y = x</u>, on the same diagram.

d) <u>Reflect</u> PQRS in the line y = x.

e) Under this transformation, what are the reflected points P′, Q′, R′ and S′?

f) Write a sentence, or show by example, what happens to the x and y coordinates <u>when reflected in the line y = x</u>.

Q8

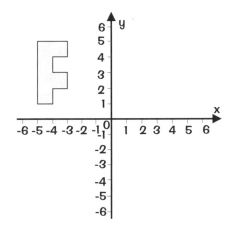

a) Draw the image of F after a rotation through 90° anti-clockwise about (0,0).

b) Start again with the original F and rotate it through 180° about (0,0). Call the image F_2.

c) How would you transform F_2 back to the original F?

Q9 <u>Describe fully</u> the transformations which place:

a) A onto E

b) A onto D

c) D onto B

d) D onto C

e) B onto F

f) F onto B

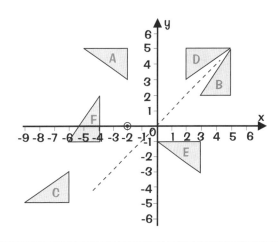

Questions on Shapes You Need To Know

You need to know about <u>all</u> of the following shapes <u>and</u> their symmetries.

Eeeek.

2-D Shapes	3-D Solids
1) SQUARE	1) REGULAR TETRAHEDRON
2) RECTANGLE	2) CYLINDER
3) RHOMBUS	3) CUBE
4) PARALLELOGRAM	4) CUBOID
5) TRAPEZIUM	5) SPHERE
6) KITE	6) TRIANGULAR PRISM
7) EQUILATERAL TRIANGLE	7) CONE
8) RIGHT-ANGLED TRIANGLE	8) SQUARE-BASED PYRAMID
9) ISOSCELES TRIANGLE	

Q1 Solve these simple riddles to find the names of 6 common shapes:

a) I have 4 sides of the same length but my two pairs of <u>parallel</u> sides are not at right angles to each other, although my <u>diagonals</u> bisect each other at 90°.

b) I am a shape that likes to fly. My two <u>isosceles</u> triangles form the four-sided shape, but if I am split down my line of symmetry I will show two <u>congruent</u> triangles instead.

c) I have four sides, 2 pairs of parallel sides, each pair of equal length but different from the other pair. I have no line of symmetry because of this and the fact that my sides don't meet at 90°.

d) I am related to a square — but I am not one.
I am related to a parallelogram — but I am not one.
I have two symmetries of <u>order 2</u>.

e) I can be one of three.
I can look like the roof of a house with a line of symmetry.
I can be one even if you join my pair of parallel sides, by any old straight lines.

f) My order of rotational symmetry = My number of lines of symmetry = My number of sides = My number of right angles.

Q2 Name 4 different triangles and draw a sketch for each one, showing appropriate, relevant differences.

Q3 Name each of the following solids. Draw in a single <u>plane</u> of symmetry if any exist:

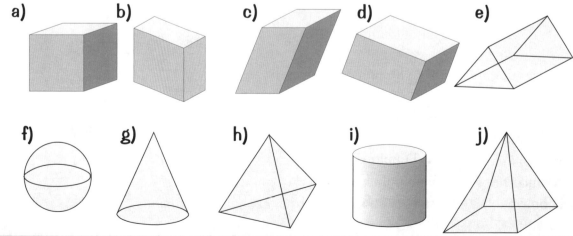

a)   b)   c)   d)   e)   f)   g)   h)   i)   j)

Questions on Circles

The Circumference C of a circle is $C = \pi \times D$

Q1 Find the <u>circumference</u> of each of the circles to 1 d.p., using $\pi = 3.14$,
   a) diameter = 20 m
   b) diameter = 12 m
   c) radius = 6 m
   d) radius = 10 m.

Q2 Taking π as the value given by your calculator, find the <u>radius</u> of the following circles. All answers to 4 d.p.
   a) Circumference of 10 m.
   b) Circumference of 0.02 mm.

Q3 Find the <u>perimeter</u> of each of the shapes drawn here. Use $\pi = 3.14$.
   a)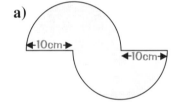
   b)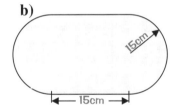
   c)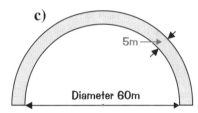

Q4 The lid on a jar of make up has a diameter of 84 mm. Using $\pi = 3.14$, what is its <u>circumference</u>?

Q5 A circular pond has a circumference of 87.92 m. Using $\pi = 3.14$ calculate its <u>diameter</u>.

Q6 A car wheel plus tyre has a diameter of 58 cm. Using $\pi = 3.14$ what is the <u>circumference</u> of the tyre? How many <u>revolutions</u> (to the nearest whole number) will the tyre make in travelling 1000 m?

Q7 A yo-yo is made up of two identical halves. Each half is circular with a circular spindle protruding from it. The two spindles are glued together and the string is tied on and wrapped around it 50 times.
   a) The central spindle has a diameter of 1.2 cm.
      What is its <u>circumference</u>?
   b) Using your answer from a), find approximately <u>how long</u> the yo-yo's string should be if 6 cm is allowed for a finger loop, and 5cm is allowed to tie it to the spindle.

Q8 A Big Wheel at a fairground has a diameter of 36 m.
   a) How far does a passenger travel in <u>one revolution</u>?
   b) If the wheel at full capacity has a speed of 6 revolutions per minute, and a ride lasts for 4 minutes, how far does a passenger travel? ($\pi = 3.14$)

STAGE ONE

Questions on Geometry

Angle Rules — you've already met a couple of these in the Polygons bit... and here are another 7 to go at. You can't get away without knowing these, I'm afraid, so get learning.

1) Angles in a triangle add up to 180°

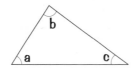

2) Angles in a 4-sided shape add up to 360°

3) Angles round a point add up to 360°

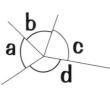

4) When a line crosses TWO PARALLEL LINES, the two bunches of angles are the same

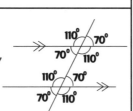

5) Angles on a straight line add up to 180°

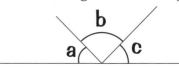

6) ISOSCELES TRIANGLES have two sides the same and two angles the same

7) In an IRREGULAR POLYGON,

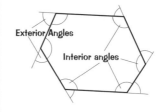

(n is the number of sides)

For the following diagrams, find the lettered angles. LM is a straight line.

Q1 a)   **b)**   **c)**   **d)**

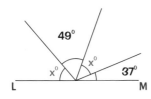

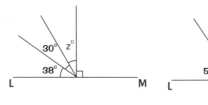

Q2 a)   **b)**   **c)**   **d)**

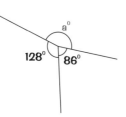

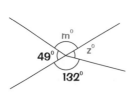

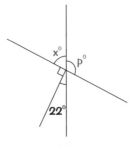

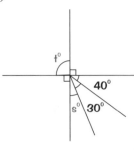

Questions on Geometry

This page is a bit dull — just lots of boring angles... still, that's geometry for you. Oh and by the way, you've got to work the angles out — don't try and sneakily measure them, they're probably drawn wrong anyway...

For the following diagrams, find the <u>lettered</u> angles. LM is a straight line.

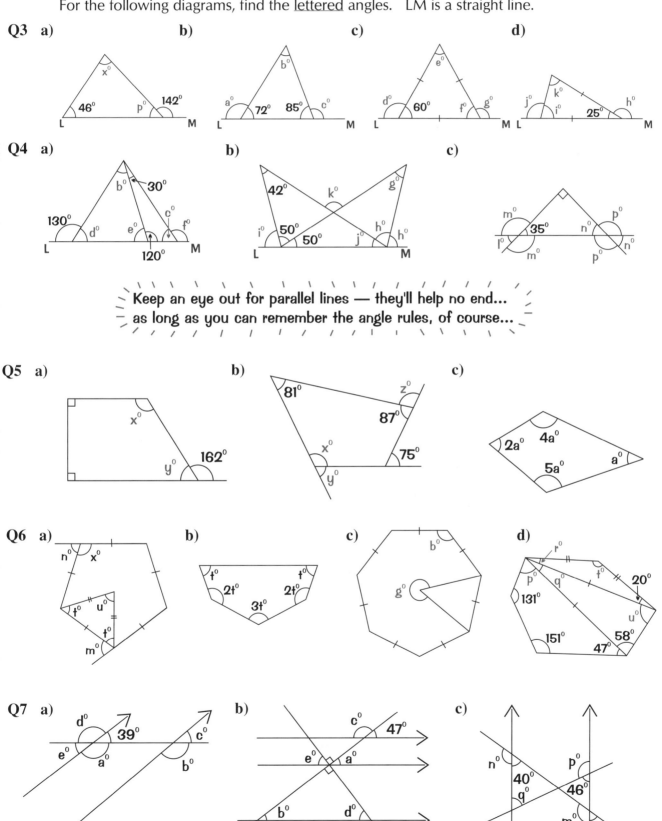

Keep an eye out for parallel lines — they'll help no end... as long as you can remember the angle rules, of course...

Questions on Bearings

~ A compass always points North...
~ It's easy to get lost here so always follow these **2 easy rules**. ~

1) **BEARINGS** are always measured clockwise **FROM** the northline.

2) You should give all bearings as **3 FIGURES**, even the small ones.

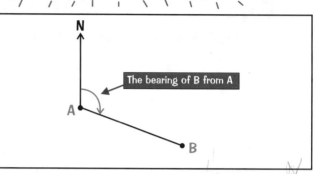

N

The bearing of B from A

A

B

Q1   State or measure the bearing of:
a) Y from X
b) X from Y
c) Z from Y
d) Y from Z.

N

105°

X

Q2   Using the same bearings as the last question, make an <u>accurate</u> scale drawing of X, Y and Z, when the distance XY is 10 km and YZ is 4 km. By <u>measurement</u> find:
a) the distance XZ
b) the bearing of Z from X
c) the bearing of X from Z.

~ You'll want to draw some extra North
~ Lines or you won't get anywhere.

Q3   This is a map of the Channel Islands.
a) Which island is furthest West?
b) Which island is due East of Guernsey? The dots show the airports.
c) What bearing is needed to fly from Jersey to Guernsey? How far is it? The flight from Jersey to Alderney goes directly over Sark.
d) What is the bearing for the first leg of the journey?
e) What is the bearing for the second leg of the journey?
f) Calculate the total distance flown from Jersey to Alderney.

Alderney

N

Guernsey   Sark

Jersey

Scale ⊢⊣ 10 miles

Q4   I live in a little village called Archam. My sister lives in the nearby village of Baddington. My sister's village is on a bearing of 135° from mine. Cowton, where my brother lives, is 10 km due west of Baddington. Cowton is 10 km due south of Archam.
a) Draw a rough sketch showing the relative positions of Archam, Baddington and Cowton.
b) What sort of shape is defined by the lines joining the three villages?
c) Calculate the area of the shape in part **b**).

Questions on Conversion Factors

The method for these questions is very easy so you might as well learn it...

> 1) Find the <u>Conversion Factor</u> *(always easy)*
> 2) <u>Multiply by it AND divide by it</u>
> 3) Choose the <u>common sense answer</u>

Q1 Cashbags Bank are offering an exchange rate of 176 Spanish Pesetas for £1 Sterling. They are also offering 7.54 French Francs for £1 Sterling and 2232 Italian Lira also for £1 Sterling. Calculate, to the nearest penny, the Sterling equivalent of:

a) 200 French Francs   **g)** 6000 Italian Lira

b) 6242 Italian Lira   **h)** 1024 Spanish Pesetas

c) 1121 Spanish Pesetas   **i)** 420 French Francs

d) 4000 Spanish Pesetas   **j)** 429 Spanish Pesetas

e) 10 French Francs   **k)** 15 French Francs

f) 19,000 Italian Lira   **l)** 1 Italian Lira.

Remember — multiply and divide then choose your answer.

Using the same exchange rates, convert the following amounts into French Francs:

m) £100

n) 200 Italian Lira

o) 300 Spanish Peseta

p) 2923 Italian Lira.

Again, using the same exchange rates, convert the following amounts into Italian Lira:

q) £100

r) 629 French Francs

s) 20 Spanish Pesetas

t) 10 French Francs.

Q2 Bryan is going to Switzerland on business.
He exchanges £500 into Swiss Francs at a rate of £1 = 2.34 Swiss Francs.

a) How many Swiss Francs does he receive?
At the last minute the trip is cancelled, so Bryan exchanges the Swiss Francs back into pounds and pence. The exchange rate is now £1 = 2.44 Swiss Francs.

b) Does Bryan make a profit or a loss?

c) To the nearest penny, how much money does Bryan gain/lose?

> 1 pint=0.568 litres
> £1=$1.42

Q3 Which is better value, 2 pints of orange juice for $0.72 or 1 litre of orange juice for 49p?

Questions on Bar Charts

These are bit of a doddle — all you do is put the
information given in different sized bars.

Q1 A group of children were asked which sports they had played at school
that day. The results are shown here:

Number of children	12	17	20	8	15
Type of Game	Basketball	Hockey	Rounders	Football	Tennis

a) Put this information in a bar chart.
b) What game was least common?
c) How many children played games?

d) How many more did hockey than football?
e) What is the range of the distrubution?
f) What was the most common game?

Q2 In the old days, wages were not as high as they are now. Below is a table showing daily
wages in shillings (approximately 5 pence).

Daily Wage (shillings)	20-30	31-40	41-50	51-60	61-70	71-80	81-90
Number of Workers	4	60	72	20	8	6	3

a) Show this information on a bar chart.
b) What wage group contains the mode?
c) What group contains the median wage for this data?
d) By setting out the information in a new table and using mid interval values, calculate an
estimate for the mean to the nearest shilling.
e) Can you tell from the data how many workers earned 45 shillings?
If so, how? If not, why not?

Q3 Thirty students were asked what their favourite chocolate bar was, out of
Maas (M), Trix (T), Kit-Kit (K), Llama bar (L) or Fudgey (F).
Tabulate the results below in a tally chart, then record them in a bar chart.

M	L	T	L	F	L	M	T	L	M
T	F	K	F	F	L	F	K	T	L
L	M	L	M	M	M	F	L	K	K

What is the modal chocolate bar?

Q4

Number of Heads	Number of Tosses (frequency)
0	5
1	11
2	17
3	32
4	20
5	9
6	6
Total	

The results of tossing six coins 100 times
were recorded by saying how many
heads were showing, after the coins had
landed. Represent this information in a
bar chart and state or calculate the
mean, range, mode and median. With
reference to any or all of this information
are the coins unbiased?

Questions on Bar Charts and Pictograms

This all seems like a compilation of "The Best Statistics Questions in the World...Ever". It'll never make the charts.

Q1 Shown below are tyre sales figures collected over a 3 month period.

Tombo: 4500	Multiroyal: 1000
Polnud: 2250	Bechstein: 3000

Represent these sales figures by drawing:
a) A <u>pictogram</u>
b) A <u>bar-line</u> graph.

Q2 The <u>grading for skiers</u> to be awarded certificates is as follows:
B - beginner, I - intermediate, G - good, VG - very good, R - racer.

To clarify the situation for a school group travelling to the Alps, the ski company would like a <u>table and a chart</u> to show the information as clearly as possible.

B	I	B	I	R	VG	I
I	R	G	VG	VG	B	B
I	I	B	B	R	B	G
I	B	G	G	I	I	I

a) What sort of <u>table</u> can you suggest? Draw it accurately.
b) What sort of <u>chart</u> would be appropriate? Draw it accurately.
c) What is the <u>most common</u> type of skier?

Q3 Answer the following questions about this <u>pictogram</u>.
a) How many lorries were sold in <u>1998</u>?
b) In which year were the <u>most</u> lorries sold?
c) How many lorries were sold in <u>1997</u>?
d) Estimate how many lorries were sold over <u>all 5 years</u>.

Sales of Lorries in 1994 → 1998

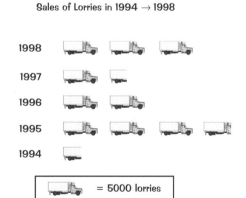

Q4 The statement "<u>cheese sales</u> are <u>increasing year on year</u>, at a <u>phenomenal rate</u>" was recently released by a cheese manufacturer, along with the graph shown on the right.
Which <u>features</u> would you <u>change</u> about this graph, so that it shows <u>more obviously</u> the <u>huge increase</u> in cheese sales over the past few years?

Questions on Simple Probability

Simple probability is simple and compound probability is harder. Well OK, the probability is you don't like either of them, but you've got to learn them anyway.

PROBABILITIES are always between 0 and 1

1) You should express probabilities as a <u>fraction</u> or a <u>decimal</u>.
2) A probability of <u>ZERO</u> means that it will <u>definitely not</u> happen.
3) A probability of <u>ONE</u> means it will <u>definitely</u> happen.

Q1 The number line opposite is a <u>probability scale</u>. Place the letters where you think the following statements lie, in terms of the <u>chance</u> of the event happening.

```
0              ½              1
```

a) The probability of getting a <u>head</u> on a toss of a 10p piece.

b) The probability of <u>choosing a red ball</u> from a bag containing 2 red balls and 1 green ball.

c) The probability of rolling a <u>five</u> on an ordinary die.

d) The probability of choosing a <u>Guatemalan stamp</u> from a bag containing 60 British stamps and 40 French stamps.

e) The probability that the <u>weather forecast</u> is correct is 25%.

f) The probability of the sun setting in the <u>West</u>, in Britain.

Q2 An ordinary die is thrown. What is the probability that it shows:

a) a 2

b) a <u>factor</u> of 12

c) an <u>odd</u> number

d) a <u>prime</u> number?

You've already done turning percentages into decimals so part e) should be no problem.

Just write down which numbers are odd, prime or factors of 12 and put this number over the total number of possibilities.

Q3 A V8 is a type of car engine with eight cylinders firing in sequence. If a V8 engine splutters it could be 'missing' on <u>any one</u> of the cylinders. What are the chances of it 'missing' on cylinder <u>number 1</u>?

Q4 In a game of Bingo, what are the chances of pulling out the <u>15</u> ball when a ball is drawn <u>at random</u> from the machine containing the balls <u>1 to 49 inclusive</u>?

SHORTHAND NOTATION

1) <u>P(x) = 0.25</u> simply means "<u>the probability of event x happening is 0.25</u>".
2) Eg: if you roll a dice, the <u>probability of rolling a 6</u> will be written as <u>P(rolls a 6)</u>.

Q5 After <u>49 tosses</u> of an unbiased coin, 24 have been heads and 25 have been tails. What is <u>P(50th toss will be a head)</u>?

Q6 A hexagonal spinner is numbered from <u>2 to 7</u>, with <u>consecutive</u> numbers. The spinner is spun and lands with its edge on the table. Find the following probabilities:

a) P(shows the number <u>2</u>)

b) P(shows an <u>odd</u> number)

c) P(shows a <u>prime</u> number)

d) P(shows a factor of 12).

The important thing to look for is the number of sides — how many <u>possibilities</u> there are.

Questions on Compound Probability

 "Compound" or "Combined" Probability is when there are two or more events. Get stuck into this little lot...

Q1 The probability of it raining during the monsoon is ¾, on a particular day.
   a) What is the probability of it <u>not raining</u>?
   b) If a monsoon 'season' lasts approximately <u>100 days</u>, how many days are likely to be <u>dry</u>?

Q2 In a lottery <u>2000</u> tickets are sold. If Mr Winter buys <u>2 tickets</u> what are the chances of him winning the single prize? If Mrs Winter buys <u>10 tickets</u> what are her chances of winning? If Mr and Mrs Winter decide to 'pool' their tickets they have <u>12 chances of winning</u> the single first prize. Work out the probability that the Winter household will <u>not</u> win the first prize.

Q3 One letter is to be chosen from the word '<u>military</u>'. What is the probability that it will be:
   a) the letter r?
   b) the letter i?
   c) a <u>vowel</u>?
   d) a <u>consonant</u>?
   e) a letter m <u>or</u> an l?

   All you need to know for part a) is how many r's are there and how many letters altogether. It'll help if you draw a little table.

Q4 An unbiased six sided die is to be thrown and then a three-colour spinner is to be spun. The die has sides numbered 1, 1, 2, 3, 4, 5 and the spinner has equal sections for red and yellow, but ½ the spinner is blue.
   a) Complete the table to show the <u>possible outcomes</u>.
   b) What is the <u>most likely</u> outcome?
   c) What is the <u>probability</u> of this outcome?
   d) What is the <u>probability (R, even)</u>?
   e) What is the <u>probability (any colour, 5)</u>?

Die → Spinner ↓	1	1	2	3	4	5
Red	(R,1)					
Yellow	(Y,1)				(Y,4)	
Blue	(B,1)					
Blue	(B,1)					

Q5 A four edged spinner has numbers 6, 7, 8 and 9. A three edged spinner has numbers 3, 4 and 5 on it.
   a) Complete the table to show all the possible scores when both spinners are spun together and their scores <u>multiplied</u>.
   b) What is the probability of achieving the <u>maximum</u> score?
   c) What is the probability of achieving an <u>odd score</u>?
   d) What is the probability of scoring a <u>multiple of 3</u>?
   e) What is the probability of scoring a <u>multiple of 10</u>?
   f) What is the probability of scoring a <u>factor of 60</u>?

X	6	7	8	9
3				
4				
5				

STAGE TWO

Questions on Rounding Off

There are two ways of choosing where to round a number off — Decimal Places is the easiest.

The Basic Method Has Three Steps

1) <u>Identify</u> the position of the LAST DIGIT.
2) Then look at the <u>next digit to the RIGHT</u> — called the DECIDER.
3) If the DECIDER is <u>5 or more</u>, then ROUND-UP the LAST DIGIT.
   If the DECIDER is <u>4 or less</u>, then leave the LAST DIGIT as it is.

Q1   David divides £15.20 by 3. What is the answer to the nearest penny?

Q2   A bumper bag of icing sugar weighs 23.4 kg. What is this correct to the nearest kilogram?

Q3   The great racing driver Speedy Wheelman covered 234.65 miles during the course of one of his races. Give this distance correct to the nearest mile.

Q4   Pru measured the length of her bedroom as 2.345 metres. Give this measurement correct to the nearest centimetre.

DP, D.P., dp, d.p., all mean the same thing — the number of <u>digits</u> to the <u>right</u> of the <u>decimal point</u>.	eg 51.35724 rounded to 4 DP will be 51.357<u>2</u> rounded to 3 D.P. will be 51.35<u>7</u> rounded to 2 dp will be 51.3<u>6</u> rounded to 1 d.p. will be 51.<u>4</u>

Q5   Round these numbers to the required number of decimal places:

a) 62.1935 (1 dp)
b) 62.1935 (2 dp)
c) 62.1935 (3 dp)
d) 19.624328 (5 dp)
e) 6.2999 (3 dp)
f) π (3 dp)

Q6   Express the following as decimals correct to 3 decimal places:

a) $\frac{1}{3}$

b) $\frac{2}{7}$

c) $\frac{5}{9}$

d) $\frac{5}{11}$

e) $3\frac{4}{13}$

f) $5\frac{4}{17}$

g) $1\frac{3}{19}$

h) $717\frac{7}{17}$

Q7   A rectangular rug is 1.6 m long and 0.6 m wide. Both measurements are given correct to one decimal place.
a) State the maximum possible length of the rug.
b) Calculate the maximum possible area of the rug.

Q8   Claudia ran a 100 m race in 11.6 seconds. If the time was measured to the nearest 0.1 seconds and the distance to the nearest metre, what is the maximum value of her average speed, in metres per second?

Questions on Accuracy and Estimating

1) For fairly _CASUAL MEASUREMENTS, 2 SIGNIFICANT FIGURES_ are most appropriate.

Cooking — 250 g (2 sig fig) of sugar, not 253 g (3 SF) or 300 g (1 SF)

2) For _IMPORTANT OR TECHNICAL THINGS, 3 SIGNIFICANT FIGURES_ are essential.

A length that will be cut to fit, eg you'd measure a shelf as 25.6 cm long, not 26 cm or 25.63 cm.

3) Only for _REALLY SCIENTIFIC WORK_ would you need over _3 SIGNIFICANT FIGURES_.

Only someone really keen would want to know the length of a piece of
string to the nearest tenth of a millimetre — like 34.46 cm, for example.

Q1   A village green is roughly rectangular with a length of 33 m 48 cm and is 24 m and 13 cm
wide. Calculate the area of the green in m², giving your answer to:
a) 2 DP
b) 3 SF.
c) State which of parts a) and b) would be the more reasonable value to use.

Just think casual, technical or really scientific...

Q2   Round each of the following to an appropriate degree of accuracy:
a) 42.798 g of sugar used to make a cake
b) a hall carpet of length 7.216 m
c) 3.429 g of $C_{12}H_{22}O_{11}$ (sugar) for a scientific experiment
d) 1.132 litres of lemonade used in a fruit punch
e) 0.541 miles from Jeremy's house to the nearest shop
f) 28.362 miles per gallon.

Q3   Calculate, giving your answer to an
appropriate degree of accuracy:

a) $\dfrac{41.75 \times 0.9784}{22.3 \times 2.54}$

b) $\dfrac{12.54 + 7.33}{12.54 - 7.22}$

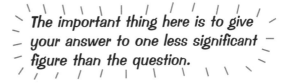

_The important thing here is to give
your answer to one less significant
figure than the question._

Q4   Estimate the volume of:
a)

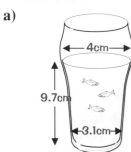

b)

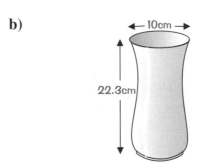

Questions on Standard Index Form

Top Tips

Writing very big (or very small) numbers gets a bit messy with all those zeros, if you don't use this standard index form. But of course, the main reason for knowing about standard form is... you guessed it — it's in the Exam.

Any numbers written in Standard Index Form <u>always</u> look like:

This number must be between 1 and 10 but never equal to 10

$$a \times 10^n$$

This number is equal to the number of places the decimal point moves.
n is +ve for larger numbers
n is -ve for small numbers

eg.
$58000000000000000 = 5.8 \times 10^{17}$
$43000000000000000000 = 4.3 \times 10^{19}$
$0.000000000000017 = 1.7 \times 10^{-15}$
$0.00000000000000008 = 8 \times 10^{-17}$

Q1 Complete these two tables.

Number	Standard form
4500000000	
19300000000000	
	8.2×10^{12}
82000000	
	6.34×10^8
	4.02×10^6
423400000000	
	8.431×10^7
	1.03×10^5
4700	

Number	Standard form
0.000000006	
0.00000000072	
	8.5×10^{-6}
0.000000143	
	7.12×10^{-5}
	3.68×10^{-10}
	4.003×10^{-8}
0.0000009321	
	5.2×10^{-3}
	9.999×10^{-7}
0.00000000802	
	2.3104×10^{-6}
0.000001	

Q2 Rewrite the following, either in standard form or changing standard form to normal numbers.

a) Mercury is 694000000 km from the Sun.

b) The Sahara desert covers 8600000 km^2.

c) The Earth is approximately 4.5×10^9 years old.

d) The average depth of the Atlantic is 3.7×10^3 miles.

e) The charge on an electron is 1.6×10^{-19} Coulombs.

f) Splitting a Uranium atom releases about 3.20×10^{-11} Joules of energy.

g) In Chemistry, Avogadro's constant is 6.033×10^{23}.

h) The circumference of the equator is 40076 km.

i) The population of the USA is approximately 249231000 people.

j) From Washington to Tokyo is 6763 miles.

k) A tonne of coal can produce 2.8×10^{10} Joules of energy.

l) The radius of a hydrogen nucleus is 0.0000000000001 cm.

m) In 2050 the population of the World will be around 1.1×10^{10} people.

You may have noticed standard form is used a lot in science, so if you're a budding nuclear physicist, get learning. Oh, you're not. Well, you've still got to learn it. Sorry.

Questions on Ratios

I don't want to spoil the surprise, but you're going to need your calculator for this bit — get your finger on that fraction button...

RATIOS are like FRACTIONS which are like DECIMALS

We can treat the RATIO 3:4 like the FRACTION ¾ which is 0.75 as a DECIMAL.

Watch out though — this isn't ¾ of the total:
If there are girls and boys in the ratio **3:4**, it means there's ¾ as many girls as boys.
So if there's 8 boys, there's ¾ × 8 = 6 girls.

Q1 Write these ratios in their simplest forms:
- **a)** 6:8
- **b)** 5:20
- **c)** 1.5:3
- **d)** 2 ¼: 4
- **e)** 2 weeks: 4 days
- **f)** £1.26:14p

Q2 A rectangle has sides in the ratio 1:2. Calculate the length of the longer side if the shorter side is:
- **a)** 3 cm
- **b)** 5.5 cm
- **c)** 15.2 m

Calculate the length of the shorter side if the longer side is:
- **d)** 3 cm
- **e)** 5.5 cm
- **f)** 15.2 m

Q3 Divide the following amounts in the ratio given:
- **a)** £20 in the ratio 2:3
- **b)** 150 m in the ratio 8:7
- **c)** 500 g in the ratio 1:2:2
- **d)** 8 hrs in the ratio 1:2:3

For questions like this — you add up the ratio numbers to find the total number of parts and divide by this. Then multiply by each number in the ratio separately to find the different amounts.

Q4 **a)** Increase £3.20 in the ratio 2:3.
b) Decrease 120 cm in the ratio 3:2.

Q5 John and Peter share a bar of chocolate marked into 16 squares. They share it in the ratio 1:3. How many squares does each boy get?

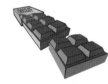

Q6

A 2 litre bottle of cola is to be shared between three girls in the ratio 2:3:5. How many millilitres will each girl get?

Watch out for your units — you'll have to change them over for this one — and your answer should be in millilitres.

Q7 Oak and Ash saplings are planted along a roadside in the ratio 2:3 respectively. If there are 20 Oak saplings how many Ash saplings are there?

Q8 Tony gives £100 to be shared by Jane, Paul and Rosemary in ratio according to their age. Jane is 10, Paul is 12 and Rosemary 3 years old. How much will each child get?

Questions on Rearranging Formulas

Rearranging is getting the letter you want out of the
formula and making it the subject.

Example:- Rearrange the formula $p = 3q + r$ to make q the subject.

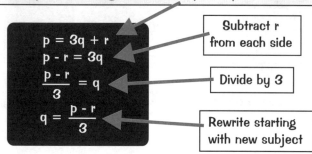

$p = 3q + r$

$p - r = 3q$

Subtract r from each side

$\dfrac{p - r}{3} = q$

Divide by 3

$q = \dfrac{p - r}{3}$

Rewrite starting with new subject

Remember
The same method applies to rearranging formulas as solving equations

Q1 Rearrange the following formulas to make the <u>letter in brackets</u> the new subject:

a) $y = x + 4$ ....(x) **f)** $s = 4t - 3$ ....(t) **k)** $y = 4 - 2x$ ....(x) **p)** $a = 3(b - 2)$ ....(b)

b) $y = 2x + 3$ ....(x) **g)** $y = 3x + \frac{1}{2}$ .....(x) **l)** $x = 8 - 3z$ ....(z) **q)** $d = \frac{1}{2}(c + 4)$ ......(c)

c) $y = 4x - 5$ ....(x) **h)** $y = 3 - x$ ....(x) **m)** $g = 10 - 4h$ ......(h) **r)** $e = 5(f - 3)$ ....(f)

d) $a = 7b + 10$ ....(b) **i)** $p = 4 - q$ ....(q) **n)** $y = 5(x + 2)$ ......(x) **s)** $g = - (h + 2)$ ....(h)

e) $w = 14 + 2z$ ...(z) **j)** $f = 12 - g$ ....(g) **o)** $s = 3(t + 4)$ ....(t) **t)** $j = -2(3 - k)$ ....(k)

Q2 Rearrange the following, to make the <u>letter in brackets</u> the subject of the formulas:

a) $y = \dfrac{x}{10}$ ....(x) **d)** $d = \dfrac{3e}{4}$ ....(e) **g)** $y = \dfrac{x}{2} - 3$ ......(x)

b) $s = \dfrac{t}{14}$ ....(t) **e)** $f = \dfrac{3g}{8}$ ....(g) **h)** $a = \dfrac{b}{3} - 5$ .....(b)

c) $a = \dfrac{2b}{3}$ ....(b) **f)** $y = \dfrac{x}{5} + 1$ ...(x) **i)** $c = \dfrac{d}{4} + 3$ ....(d)

Q3 A car sales person is paid £w for working m months and selling c cars, where
$w = 500m + 50c$.

a) Rearrange the formula to make <u>c the subject</u>.

b) Find the number of cars the sales person sells in 11 months if he earns £12,100 during that
time.

Q4 The cost of hiring a spacetaxi is £28 for each <u>whole</u> light year
plus 25p per extra mile. (A light year is the <u>distance</u> light
travels in a year. So it's very <u>large</u>.)

a) Find the cost of hiring the spacetaxi and travelling
  i) 1 light year and 40 miles **ii)** 1 light year and 80 miles

b) Write down a formula to give £c the cost of hiring a spacetaxi,
in pounds, for travelling one light year and n miles.

c) Rearrange the formula to make <u>n the subject</u>.

d) What is the furthest you can travel on this amount of money?
  i) £34   **ii)** £50   **iii)** £56.50

Q5 The rectangle has length l cm and width w cm. Its perimeter is p cm.

a) Write down a <u>formula</u> with p as the subject.

b) Rearrange this to make l the subject.

c) Find the length of a rectangle of width 7.5 cm and perimeter 44 cm.

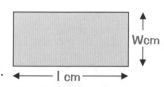

Wcm

l cm

STAGE TWO

Questions on Inequalities

Yet another one of those bits of Maths that looks worse than it is
— these are just like equations, really, except for the symbols.

The 4 Inequality Symbols:

> means greater than   < means less than
⩾ means greater than or equal to   ⩽ means less than or equal to

Inequalities can be represented on number lines. You need to know this notation, too:

Eg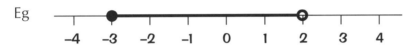

REMEMBER:
● includes the value
○ does not include it

represents the inequality $-3 \leqslant x < 2$

Q1 Write down an inequality for each of the diagrams below.

a) 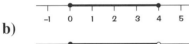   g)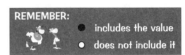

b)    h)

c)    i)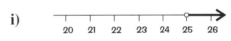

d)    j)

e)    k)

f)   l)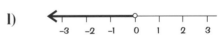

Q2 For each of the following, draw and label a number line from _−5 to 5_ and use it to represent the inequality:

a) $x^2 \leqslant 4$ c) $x^2 \leqslant 9$ e) $16 \geqslant x^2$ g) $9 > x^2$
b) $x^2 < 1$ d) $25 \geqslant x^2$ f) $x^2 \leqslant 1$ h) $x^2 \leqslant 0$

Q3 Solve the following inequalities:

a) $2x \geqslant 16$ f) $10x > -2$ k) $5x + 4 < 24$
b) $4x > -20$ g) $5 + x \geqslant 12$ l) $5x + 7 \leqslant 32$
c) $x + 2 > 5$ h) $x/4 > 10$ m) $3x + 12 \leqslant 30$
d) $x - 3 \leqslant 10$ i) $x/3 \leqslant 1$ n) $2x - 7 \geqslant 8$
e) $x + 4 \geqslant 14$ j) $x/2 \leqslant 4$ o) $17 + 4x < 33$

Q4 There are _1,130_ pupils in a school and no classes have more than _32_ pupils. How many _classrooms_ could be used? Show this information as an inequality.

Q5 A person is prepared to spend _£300_ taking friends out to celebrate. If the restaurant charges _£12 per head_, how many guests could be invited? Show this information as an inequality.

Questions on Trial and Improvement

Solving a Cubic Equation

Eg The cubic equation $x^3 + 2x = 15$ has a solution between 2 and 3. Find this to 1 d.p.

Guess (x)	value of x^3+2x	Too large or too small
2	$2^3+2(2)=12$	Too small
3	$3^3+2(3)=33$	Too large
2.3	$(2.3)^3+2(2.3)=16.767$	Too large
2.2	$(2.2)^3+2(2.2)=15.048$	Too large ...Just!
2.1	$(2.1)^3+2(2.1)=13.461$	Too small
2.15	$(2.15)^3+2(2.15)=14.238$	Too small

2 gave an answer closer to 15 so the next guess should be nearer to 2 than 3.

In this example it looks like x=2.2, but to be totally sure, always try exactly halfway when you reach this stage.

∴ To 1 d.p the solution is <u>x=2.2</u>

Q1   The cubic equation $x^3 + x = 24$ has a solution between 2 and 3.
Copy and complete the table below and use it to find this solution to <u>1 DP</u>.

Guess (x)	value of x^3+x	Too large or too small
2	$2^3+2=$	
3	$3^3+3=$	

Extend the table as necessary

Q2   The cubic equation $x^3 - x = 34$ has a solution between 3 and 4.
Copy and complete the table below and use it to find this solution to <u>1 DP</u>.

Guess (x)	value of $x^3- x$	Too large or too small
3	$3^3- 3=$	
4	$4^3- 4=$	

Q3   The cubic equation $2x^3 - x^2 = 50$ has a solution between 3 and 4. Use the table to find this solution to <u>1 DP</u>.

Guess (x)	value of $2x^3- x^2$	Too large or too small
3	$2(3)^3- (3)^2 =$	
4	$2(4)^3- (4)^2 =$	

top tip

Questions on Straight Line Graphs

The <u>very first thing</u> you've got to do is work out a <u>table of values</u>.

Example: Draw the graph of y = 3x – 1 for values of x
between 0 and 4.

1) First complete a <u>table of values</u>:

x	0	1	2	3	4
y	-1	2	5	8	11

⇐ decided by the question

⇐ worked out using y = 3x - 1

2) Draw the axes.
3) Plot the points.
4) Label the line y = 3x – 1.
   (step 4 has been left for you to complete)

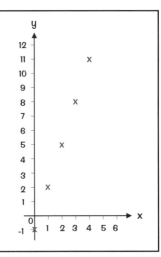

Once you know they're in a straight line, just get your ruler out and you're away.

Q1 a) Complete the table below, for y = x + 2.

x	0	1	2	3	4	5	6
y	2			5			

b) Use your <u>table of values</u> to draw the graph
y = x + 2.
c) Where does your graph cross the_Y-axis?
d) What is the <u>gradient</u> of your graph?

Q2 a) Complete the table below for y = 2x + 1.

x	0	1	2	3	4	5	6
y	1				9		

b) Use your table of values to draw the
graph y = 2x + 1.

c) Where does your graph cross the Y-axis?
d) What is the <u>gradient</u> of your graph?

The x-intercept sounds pretty fancy but all it means is the place where the line crosses the X-axis. (Same with the y-intercept.) Easy lemons.

Q3 a) Draw the graph of y = 5 – x, for values of x <u>between 0 and 6</u>.
b) Where does the graph cross the <u>Y-axis</u>?
c) What is the gradient of the graph?

Q4 By <u>drawing the graph</u> of y = 3x – 3, find where it crosses the Y-axis and the gradient.

Q5 Find the <u>y-intercept</u> (where it crosses the Y-axis) and the <u>gradient</u> of the graph y = ½x + 3.

Once you've got the hang of this bit, look at the next page. You'll need to know both ways of doing these, so be warned — you can't just pick your favourite method and stick to it. More's the pity.

Questions on Quadratic Graphs

You can write all quadratic graphs in this form — though you probably won't see the point of doing it 'till you've done quite a few of them. Hang in there.

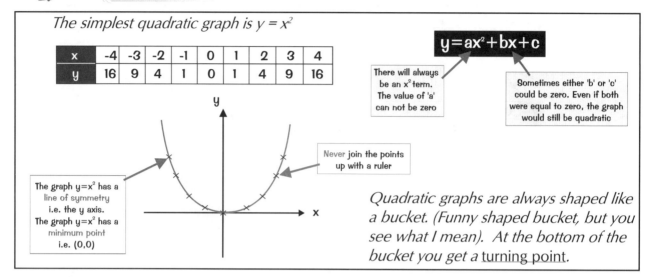

The simplest quadratic graph is $y = x^2$

x	-4	-3	-2	-1	0	1	2	3	4
y	16	9	4	1	0	1	4	9	16

$$y = ax^2 + bx + c$$

There will always be an x^2 term. The value of 'a' can not be zero

Sometimes either 'b' or 'c' could be zero. Even if both were equal to zero, the graph would still be quadratic

Never join the points up with a ruler

The graph $y = x^2$ has a line of symmetry i.e. the y axis.
The graph $y = x^2$ has a minimum point i.e. (0,0)

Quadratic graphs are always shaped like a bucket. (Funny shaped bucket, but you see what I mean). At the bottom of the bucket you get a <u>turning point</u>.

Q1 Complete this <u>table of values</u> for the quadratic graph $y = 2x^2$.

a) Draw axes with x from -4 to 4 and y from 0 to 32.

b) Plot these 9 points and join them with a <u>smooth curve</u>.

c) Label your graph.

x	-4	-3	-2	-1	0	1	2	3	4
$y = 2x^2$	32	18					8		

Remember to square first then x 2

You always get a vertical <u>line of symmetry</u> down the middle of the graph, and you can often be asked to write its equation down. Remember that a vertical line will always have the equation "x = something", the something being the number where it crosses the X-axis.

Q2 Complete this table of values for the graph $y = x^2 + x$.

x	-4	-3	-2	-1	0	1	2	3	4
x^2	16	9					8		
$y = x^2 + x$	12					2			

By putting more steps in your table of values, the arithmetic is easier

a) Draw axes with x from -4 to 4 and y from 0 to 20.

b) Plot the points and join them with a smooth curve.

c) Draw the <u>line of symmetry</u> for the quadratic graph $y = x^2 + x$, and label it.

d) Describe the <u>turning point</u> of the quadratic and state its coordinates.

If the x^2 term has a <u>minus</u> sign in front of it, the bucket will be turned <u>upside down</u>.

Q3 a) Draw the graph $y = -x^2$ for values of x from -4 to 4.

b) Describe the turning point of the graph and state its <u>coordinates</u>.

c) How are this graph and the graph $y = x^2$ (at the top of this page) related?

If you don't get the equation given in the form $y = ax^2 + bx + c$ then <u>put it in that form first</u>. You'll get in a right mess if you don't.

Questions on Quadratic Graphs

It's handy to know whether a quadratic graph will have a <u>maximum point</u> or a <u>minimum point</u> without having to plot the graph first. This is how you know:

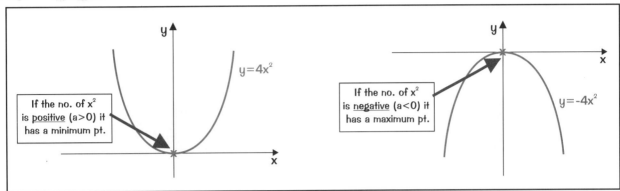

<u>(If the bucket is the right way up, you get a minimum.</u>
<u>If it's upside down, you get a maximum.)</u>

Q4 **a)** Complete this table of values for the graph $y = 3 - x^2$.

   b) Draw the graph $y = 3 - x^2$ for x from -4 to 4.

   c) State the <u>maximum point</u> of the graph $y = 3 - x^2$.

   d) State the <u>maximum value</u> of the graph $y = 3 - x^2$.

x	-4	-3	-2	-1	0	1	2	3	4
3	3	3	3	3	3	3	3	3	3
$-x^2$	-16						-4		
$y=3-x^2$	-13						-1		

If you don't get a smooth curve you've screwed up.

Q5 **a)** Complete this table of values for the graph $y = x^2 - 4x + 1$.

   b) <u>Plot the graph</u> $y = x^2 - 4x + 1$, using axes with x from -2 to 5 and y from -3 to 13.

   c) Draw and label the <u>line of symmetry</u>.

   d) What is the minimum value of the graph $y = x^2 - 4x + 1$?

x	-2	-1	0	1	2	3	4
x^2	4	1				9	
-4x	8					-12	
1	1	1				1	
$y=x^2-4x+1$	13	6				-2	

Q6 <u>Without drawing their graphs</u>, determine whether these quadratic graphs will have maximum points or minimum points.

   a) $y = 2x^2 - 5$ **c)** $y = 4x - 3x^2$

   b) $y = 10 - x^2$ **d)** $y = 5 - 3x + x^2$.

Q7 **a)** Draw axes with x from -3 to 5 and y from -9 to 7.

   b) By first completing the table of values, plot the graph $y = x^2 - 2x - 8$.

   c) State the line of symmetry.

   d) <u>Describe the turning point</u> and state its coordinates.

x			
x^2			
-2x			
-8			
$y=x^2-2x-8$			

If any points look a bit strange, check you've got them right in the <u>table of values</u>. I know it's boring doing it all again, but it shouldn't be too hard if you've put all the steps in. And it'll mean you <u>don't get it wrong</u>. Which is always nice.

STAGE TWO

Questions on Real Life Graphs

Conversion graphs let you swap from one unit to another,
just by reading the graph — what fun.

Q1   Using the <u>conversion graph</u> convert the following
to km, rounding your answers to the <u>nearest km</u>:

a) 5 miles   **c)** 11 miles
b) 20 miles   **d)** 23 miles.

Q2   Change the following to <u>miles</u>, rounding your
answers to the nearest mile:

a) 10 km   **c)** 27 km
b) 20 km   **d)** 35 km.

Q3   Find the <u>gradient</u> of the graph.

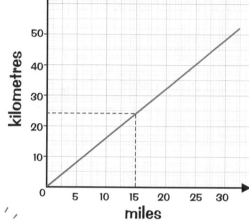

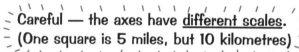
Careful — the axes have <u>different scales</u>.
(One square is 5 miles, but 10 kilometres)

Q4   Using the conversion graph on the right, change
the following to <u>°C</u>:

a) 40°F   **c)** 75°F
b) 60°F   **d)** 120°F

Q5   Using the conversion graph change the
following to <u>°F</u>:

a) 10°C   **c)** 40°C
b) 28°C   **d)** 48°C

Q6   A person's normal body temperature is 98.4°F.
What is this <u>approximately in °C</u>?

OK, this next question's a bit of a toughie, but at
least there's some help on how to draw the graph.

Q7   To draw a conversion graph to change <u>£ into $</u>, you will need to:
-draw the £ axis horizontally and label it from 0 to 10 (1 cm for every pound).
-draw the $ axis vertically and label it from 0 to 16 (1 cm for every dollar).
-plot the point representing <u>£10 in dollars</u>, given that the <u>exchange rate</u> is 1.6 dollars to the
pound, and join this to the origin with a straight line.

From your graph find:
a) how many dollars you would receive if you exchanged £7.
b) how many pounds you would receive if you exchanged $6.
   If the strength of the pound increased you would need to adjust this conversion graph.
c) Would the adjusted conversion graph's <u>gradient</u> be <u>greater or less</u>
   than the original graph's gradient?

For that last bit, remember that when the strength of the
pound <u>increases</u>, you get <u>more dollars</u> for your pound.

STAGE TWO

Questions on Real Life Graphs

Sometimes they'll only want the <u>shape</u> of a graph, so you can just <u>sketch</u> it. A sketch graph doesn't have any points plotted, but you still need to draw a pair of labelled axes (with a ruler, of course).

Q8 Show the general relationship between these quantities by <u>sketching</u> a graph for each case. Place the <u>first</u> quantity mentioned on the <u>Y-axis</u>.

a) The <u>level of water</u> in a rectangular tank when drained at a constant rate, <u>against time</u>.

b) The <u>volumes of cubes</u> with edges of different lengths.

c) The <u>amount</u> raised <u>per mile</u> on a sponsored walk.

d) The <u>area</u> of an <u>equilateral triangle</u> compared to the length of an edge.

When you're doing these questions, ask yourself these three main things:—

1) is it a straight line or a curved one?
2) will the line be horizontal, vertical, uphill or downhill?
3) will it cross either of the axes and if it does, will it be left, right, above or below the origin?

Q9 Match the following sketches with the statements below:

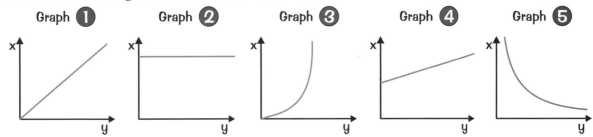

Graph ❶ Graph ❷ Graph ❸ Graph ❹ Graph ❺

a) The graph is showing the cost of hiring a plumber <u>per hour</u> including a <u>fixed call-out fee</u>.

b) The graph is showing the connection between the <u>length and width</u> of a rectangle of a fixed area.

c) The graph is showing <u>speed against time</u> for a car travelling at constant speed.

d) The graph is showing the <u>area of a circle</u> as the radius increases.

<u>Keep asking yourself</u> the <u>three questions</u> about what you'd expect the graph to look like, then see if any of them are in there. If they aren't, you've gone wrong, so <u>try again</u>.

Q10 Water is poured into each of these containers at a <u>constant rate</u>.

Match the containers to the graphs showing the <u>depth</u> of water (d) against <u>time</u> (t) taken to fill the container.

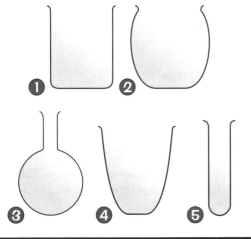

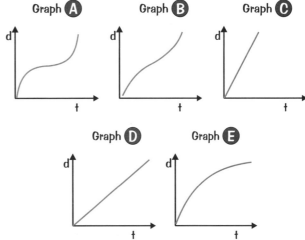

Graph Ⓐ Graph Ⓑ Graph Ⓒ

Graph Ⓓ Graph Ⓔ

Questions on Pythagoras' Theorem

If you're as big a fan of Pythagoras as me, you'll ignore him and use this method instead:

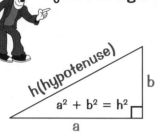

The Simple Three Step Method

1) SQUARE the two numbers that you are given.
2) To find the <u>longest side, ADD</u> the two squared numbers.
   To find a <u>shorter side, SUBTRACT</u> the smaller one from the larger.
3) Take the SQUARE ROOT. Then check that your answer is sensible.

Q1 Using Pythagoras' theorem, calculate the length of the third side in these triangles, giving your answers to <u>3 significant figures</u>.

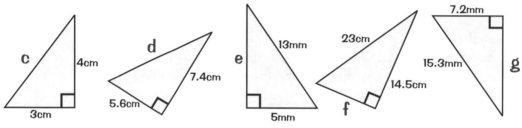

Q2 Using Pythagoras' theorem, work out which of these triangles have right-angles.

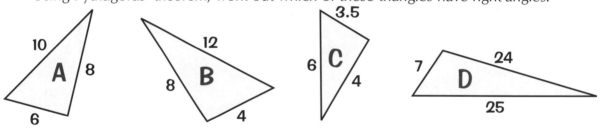

Q3 Calculate the <u>missing lengths</u> in these quadrilaterals.

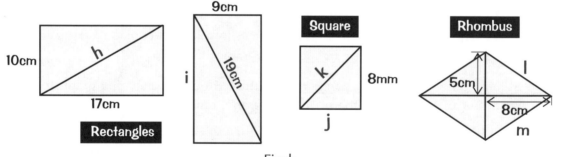

Q4

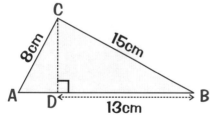

Find:
a) the height CD of this triangle
b) the length AD
c) the whole base length AB
d) the area of triangle ABC.
e) Is the triangle ABC right-angled ?

Q5 Find:
a) the length WX
b) the length WZ
c) the area of triangle WXZ.

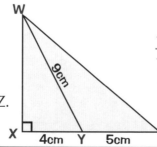

When there's more than one triangle, it's a bit harder to tell which side is which. Your best bet is to draw each triangle separately as you're using it — that way you'll get less muddled up.

STAGE TWO

Questions on Pythagoras' Theorem

You may have noticed that <u>none of these questions involve angles</u> — I guess that Mr Pythagoras wasn't too keen on them. So before you go reaching for that SIN button on your calculator, think again...

Q6 A builder has to reach the roof of a house 15 m high. His ladder is 20 m long. How far away from the house must the <u>foot of the ladder</u> be placed?

Q7

A flagpole is 6.5 m high and has 3 stay lines from the top to the ground. If the stay lines are 8, 9 and 10 m long how far from the foot of the flagpole must each one be secured?

Q8 A farmer has an oddly shaped field, as shown in the diagram, divided into two right-angled triangles. What length of fencing does he need to go all round the <u>perimeter</u> (not across the middle)?

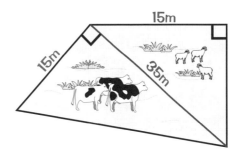

Q9

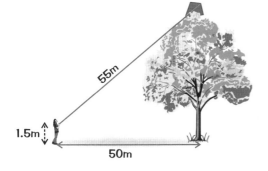

Jane was flying her kite on a string 55 m long. She is 1.5 m tall and was standing 50 m from the base of the tree. How tall must the tree be if Jane's kite could get <u>tangled in the top</u>?

Well, there's lots of practice to be had here, whether you want it or not. Still, once you've battled your way through all of these, you'll
a) be bored out of your mind
b) have another topic under your belt.

Q10 The doorway of a tent is an <u>isosceles</u> triangle. The height of the pole is 1.2 m and the distance from the base of the pole to the canvas is 56 cm. Find:

a) the length of the canvas from pole top to ground
b) the area of the doorway.

You'll be a lot better off if you draw diagrams for questions 11 & 12.

Q11 A ship leaves port and steams 100 km <u>due North</u>. It then turns and steams 120 km <u>due East</u>. How far is it from port now?

Q12 How long is the line that joins the points A (2,1) and B (8,2)?

Questions on Trigonometry

You really need to know your <u>trigonometric formulas</u> — you'll struggle without them.

An **EASY WAY** to remember the **THREE** formulas is to write **"SOH CAH TOA"** before you start — then turn the most suitable into a **FORMULA TRIANGLE**.

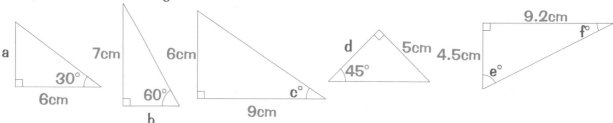

Q1   Use <u>TAN</u> to find the angle or side labelled with a letter.

  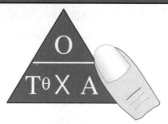

Q2   Use <u>COS</u> to find the angle or side labelled with a letter.

Don't try and do it all in your head — you're gonna have to get your pen out and label the sides. You'll find it loads easier to see what's going on.

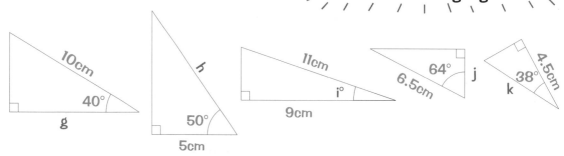

Q3   Use <u>SIN</u> to find the angle or side labelled with a letter.

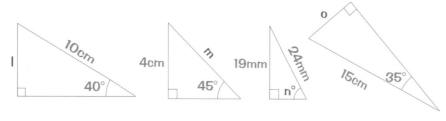

Q4   Choose the most suitable formula to find the lettered angles and sides.

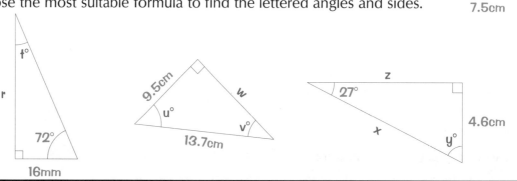

Questions on Trigonometry

Don't worry, these questions are just more of the same — except they've got prettier pictures. Don't forget to label the sides, though.

Q5 Mary was lying on the floor looking up at the star on top of her Christmas tree. She looked up through an angle of 55° when she was 1.5 m from the base of the tree. How high was the star?

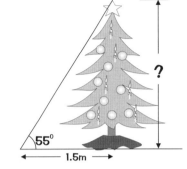

Q6 Mr Brown took his dog for a walk in the park. The dog's lead was 2 m long. The dog ran 0.7 m from the path Mr Brown was walking on.

What angle did the lead make with the path?

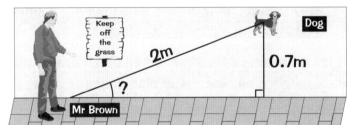

Q7 A coastguard on a cliff top saw a boat in trouble at sea. The cliff was 156 m high. The angle of depression that the coastguard looked along was 25°.

What distance was the boat from:
a) the base of the cliff?
b) the coastguard?

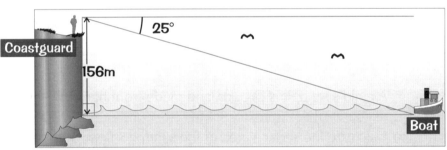

Remember, the angle of <u>depression</u> is always the <u>same</u> as the angle of <u>elevation</u>.

Q8 A boy walked diagonally across a rectangular field and measured the distance as 95 m. The line he walked on made an angle of 40° with the longer edge of the field.
a) Draw a <u>rough sketch</u> of the field and the boy's path across it.
b) Calculate the length and width of the field.
c) Calculate the area of the field.

Q9 A window cleaner with an extending ladder has to clean windows on two levels of a building. For the lower level his ladder must reach to 3.5 m. For the higher level it must reach 7 m. If the base of the ladder is always 2.5 m from the wall what angle is made with the horizontal when used for:
a) the lower level?
b) the upper level?

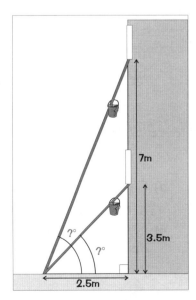

STAGE TWO

Questions on Circles

Circle Formulas

1) The Area A of a circle is $A = \pi \times r^2$

2) The <u>Circumference C</u> of a circle is $C = \pi \times D$

Q1 Using $\pi = 3.14$, find:
- **a)** The area of a circle with radius = 6.12 m. Give your answer <u>to 3 dp</u>.
- **b)** The circumference of a circle with radius = 7.2 m. Give your answer <u>to 2 sf</u>.
- **c)** The circumference of a circle with diameter = 14.8 m. Give your answer <u>to 1 dp</u>.
- **d)** The area of a circle with diameter = 4.246 cm. Give answer your <u>to 3 dp</u>.

Q2 A pond with a circumference of 87.92 m has a 1 m wide concrete path around its circumference. Calculate the <u>area of the path</u>.

Q3 A rug in front of a fire is in the shape of a semicircle. It has a diameter equal to the width of the fire hearth, which is 1.8 m wide. Using $\pi = 3.14$ calculate the <u>area of the rug</u>, to 3 sf.

Q4 The rug in Q3 is to have non-slip braid attached around its perimeter to stop it moving. How many <u>metres of braid</u> will be required to do the job? (Give answer to 3 sf.)

Q5 A child's sandpit is circular, and made from hard PVC. It has a depth of 10 cm and a diameter of 450 mm. ($\pi = 3.14$)
- **a)** Calculate the <u>surface area</u> of the sandpit's floor both in mm² and m² to 2 dp.
- **b)** A red stripe is to be painted all of the way round the inside face of the sandpit. <u>How long</u> would the stripe be in mm?
- **c)** If the stripe were to be 20 mm wide, what <u>area</u> of red paint would be visible?

Q6 The <u>base</u> of a triangle is equal in length to the <u>circumference</u> of a circle which has a radius of 5 cm. The triangle and the circle also have an <u>equal area</u>. What is the height of the triangle? (Again, $\pi = 3.14$)

Q7 The diagram shows the spool on a cassette with recording tape wrapped around it. The ring of tape has an internal radius of 11 mm and external radius 23 mm.
- **a)** Find the area of the <u>side view</u> of tape in cm².
- **b)** If the recording tape is 50 m long, how <u>thick</u> is it?
- **c)** If half of the cassette is played, half of the tape is unwound from one spool to the other. Calculate the external radius of the tape now occupying the <u>original</u> spool.

Questions on Enlargement

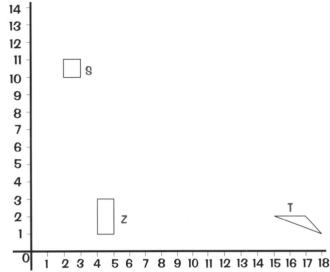

Q1 Enlarge square S by a scale factor of 4. The centre of enlargement is (2, 12). Label the new square K′ L′ M′ N′. What are the <u>coordinates</u> of these new points?

Q2 Enlarge rectangle Z by a scale factor of 3 using any method. The centre of enlargement is (2,0). Label the new rectangle W′X′Y′V′. What are the <u>coordinates</u> of these new points?

Q3 Enlarge triangle T by a scale factor of 2 about (18,0). Label this triangle T′.
Reduce T′ by a scale factor of ½ about a centre of enlargement (12,0). Label this triangle T″.
   a) Give the three coordinates of T″.
   b) What <u>single</u> transformation would map T onto T″?
   c) What <u>single</u> transformation would map T″ back onto T?

Q4 Square A1 is an enlargement of square A. Find the centre of enlargement. What is the scale factor of enlargement?

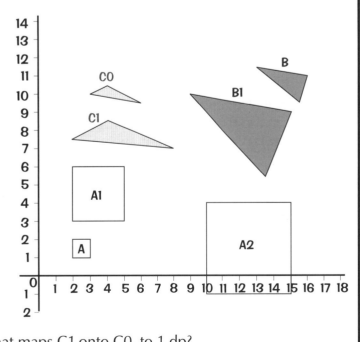

Q5 Square A2 is an <u>enlargement</u> of square A.
 Find the centre of enlargement. What are its coordinates?
 What is the scale factor of enlargement mapping A onto A2?

Q6 B1 is an <u>enlargement</u> of B.
 What are the coordinates of the centre of enlargement?
 What scale factor maps B onto B1?

Q7 C0 is a <u>reduction</u> of C1.
 Find the centre of reduction to 1 dp.
 What is the scale factor of reduction that maps C1 onto C0, to 1 dp?

Questions on Speed

This is an easy enough formula — and of course you can put it in that good old formula triangle as well.

$$\text{Average speed} = \frac{\text{Total distance}}{\text{Total time}}$$

Q1 A train travels 240 km in 4 hours. What is its <u>average speed</u>?

Q2 A car travels for 3 hours at an average speed of 55 m.p.h. How far has it travelled?

Q3 <u>Complete</u> this table.

Distance Travelled	Time taken	Average Speed
210 km	3 hrs	
135 miles		30 mph
	2 hrs 30 mins	42 km/h
9 miles	45 mins	
640 km		800 km/h
	1 hr 10 mins	60 mph

Q4 The distance from Kendal (Oxenholme) to London (Euston) is 280 miles. The train travels at an average speed of 63 m.p.h. If I catch the 07.05 from Kendal, can I be at a meeting in London by 10.30? <u>Show all your working</u>.

Q5 A plane flies over city A at 09.55 and over city B at 10.02. What is its <u>average</u> speed if these cities are 63 miles apart?

Q6 An athlete can run 100 m in 28 seconds. Calculate the athlete's speed in:
a) m/sec
b) km/hr.

Q7 In a speed trial, a sand yacht travelled a measured mile in 36.4 seconds.
a) Calculate this speed in m.p.h.
On the return mile he took 36.16 seconds.
b) Find his <u>total time</u> for the two runs.
c) Calculate the average speed in m.p.h.

> Remember, for the <u>average</u> speed, you use the <u>total</u> time and <u>total</u> distance.

Q8 A motorist drives from Manchester to London. 180 miles is on motorway, where he averages 65 m.p.h. 55 miles is on city roads, where he averages 28 m.p.h. 15 miles is on country roads, where he averages 25 m.p.h.
a) Calculate the total time taken for the journey.
b) How far did he travel altogether?
c) Calculate the average speed for the journey.

I reckon this is <u>pretty easy</u> — it's just a case of taking your time, putting the right numbers into the <u>speed formula triangle</u> and getting the answer out. And don't forget to check your answer is in the <u>right units</u>.

Questions on Density

Here we go again — the <u>multi-purpose formula triangle</u>. <u>Learn</u> the positions of <u>M, D and V</u>, plug in the <u>numbers</u> and pull out the <u>answer</u>... magic.

$$\text{DENSITY} = \frac{\text{mass}}{\text{volume}}$$

Q1 Find the <u>density</u> of each of these pieces of wood, giving your answer in g/cm³:

a) Mass 3 g, volume 4 cm³

b) Mass 12 kg, volume 20,000 cm³

c) Mass 20 g, volume 25 cm³

d) Mass 14 kg, volume 0.02 m³.

Q2 Calculate the <u>mass</u> of each of these objects:

a) a small marble statue of density 2.6 g/cm³ and volume 24 cm³

b) a plastic cube of volume 64 cm³ and density 1.5 g/cm³

c) a gold ingot measuring 12 cm by 4 cm by 4 cm with density 19.5 g/cm³

d) a pebble with volume 30 cm³ and density 2.5 g/cm³.

Q3 Work out the <u>volume</u> of each of these items:

a) a bag of sugar of mass 1 kg and density 1.6 g/cm³

b) a packet of margarine with density 2.8 g/cm³ and mass 250 g

c) a 50 kg sack of coal with density 1.8 g/cm³

d) a box of cereal with density 0.2 g/cm³ and mass 500 g.

Q4 Ice has a density of 0.93 g/cm³. If the mass of a block of ice is 19.5 kg, what is its <u>volume</u>?

Q5 The area of the Falkland Islands is 12,173 km². The 1972 census gave the population as 1,957.

a) Calculate the density of the <u>population</u> per km².

There are 635,000 sheep and 10,000 cattle on the Islands.

Work out the <u>density</u> of:

b) sheep per km²

c) cattle per km².

Q6 Some petrol in a can has a mass of 4 kg. The density of the petrol is 0.8 g/cm³. How many litres of petrol are in the can?

Q7 My copper bracelet has a volume of 3.9 cm³. The density of copper is 8.9 g/cm³. Work out the <u>mass</u> of my bracelet.

Q8 A jug holds 1.9 litres of lemonade. The mass of the lemonade is 2 kg. Find the <u>density</u> of the lemonade.

Q9 A 1.5 kg bag full of self raising flour measures 12 cm by 18 cm by 6 cm. A 1 kg bag of granary flour measures 10 cm by 14 cm by 6 cm. Find the <u>density</u> of each sort of flour.

Questions on Areas

Here's the Top 4 Formulas — if you know these you can work out just about any area.

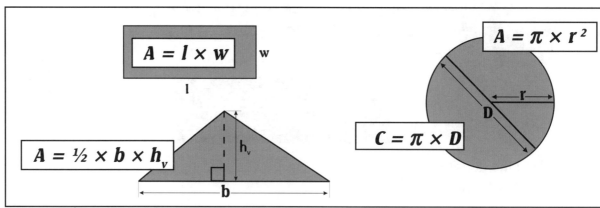

Q1 Calculate the area of the rectangle.

Q2 Calculate the area of the square.

Q3 A rectangular dining room, with a width equal to half its length, needs carpet tiling.
a) Calculate the area of the floor, if its width is 12 m.
b) If carpet tiles are 50 cm by 50 cm squares, calculate how many tiles will be required.
c) If carpet tiles cost £4.99 per m², calculate the cost of tiling the dinning room.

Q4 An attachment on a child's toy is made from plastic in the shape of an octagon with a square cut out.
By counting squares or otherwise, find the area of plastic needed to make 4 of these attachments.

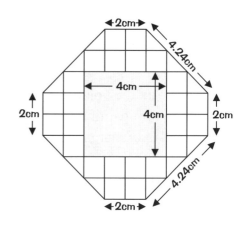

Q5 A cube bean bag is to be made out of material. If each side of the cube is to have edges of length 60 cm, how many square metres of material will be needed?

Q6 The area of a square is 9000 m².
a) What is the length of a side? (to 2 dp)
b) What is the perimeter of the square? (to 2 dp)

Q7 A fighter aircraft's wing is shown on the right. Calculate its area, and its perimeter.

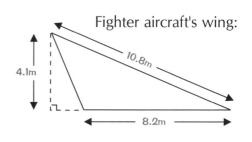

Fighter aircraft's wing:

Q8 A hanging basket bracket of sheet metal is stamped out in a 2 phase process:-
1st: The outer triangle, measuring 14.4 cm by 10 cm, is stamped out.
2nd: A smaller inner triangle measuring 5.76 cm by 4 cm is stamped out of the larger triangle.
How much metal makes up the finished bracket?

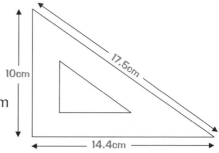

Questions on Perimeters and Areas

<u>PERIMETER</u> is the distance all the way around the outside of a 2D shape

Always use the <u>BIG BLOB</u> method :
1) Put a <u>BIG BLOB</u> at one corner, then go around the shape.
2) Write down the length of every side as you go.
3) Even sides that seem to have no length given — you must work them out.
4) Keep going until you get back to the <u>BIG BLOB</u>. Then add up all the sides.

Q1 A sail is the triangular shape shown in the diagram.
a) What is its <u>perimeter</u>?
b) A smaller sail is kept in a locker to be used on windier days.
Its area is 26.8 m², its width is 2.06 m and it is also isosceles.
  i) Find its <u>height.</u>
  ii) Find its <u>perimeter.</u>

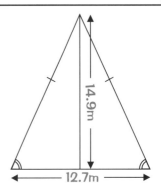

Q2 In front of a <u>toilet</u> is a special mat that fits snugly around the base.

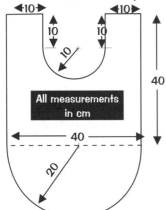

Using the diagram opposite:
a) Find the <u>length of braid</u> needed to be stitched all round its edge.
b) Find the <u>area</u> of fluffy wool carpet it will cover when placed in front of the toilet.

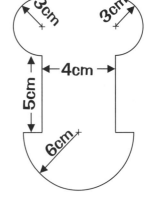

Q3 A new ergonomically designed computer mouse is shaped as shown in the diagram.
Work out the approximate surface area of the top of it.

Q4 Before angle measurers, <u>protractors</u> were used to measure angles up to 180°.
They were made of plastic with a semi circle attached to a rectangle.

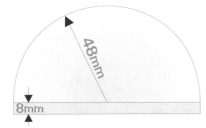

a) Calculate the <u>area of plastic</u> needed to make one.
b) If you were to draw all the way round it, <u>how long</u> would the line be?

STAGE TWO

Questions on Volume and Capacity

<u>Capacity</u> is <u>exactly</u> the same thing as <u>volume</u> — simple as that. And things will get even simpler once you've learnt the two formulas below.

VOLUME FORMULAS

1) Volume of cuboid =
   Length × Width × Height

2) Volume of any prism =
   Cross-sectional area × Length

Constant Area
of Cross-section — Length

Q1 A coffee mug is a cylinder closed at one end. The internal radius is 7 cm with an internal height of 9 cm.

   a) If $\pi = 3.14$, find the <u>volume</u> of liquid the mug can hold.

   b) If 1200 cm³ of liquid is poured into the mug, find the <u>depth</u> to the nearest whole mm.

Q2 An unsharpened pencil can be thought of as a <u>regular hexagonal prism</u> with a cylinder of graphite along the axis of the prism.

   a) By considering a hexagon to be made up of <u>six</u> <u>equilateral triangles</u>, calculate the area of the cross-section of the hexagonal prism, shown.

   b) Find the <u>area of wood</u> in the cross-section.

   c) If the pencil is 20 cm long what is the <u>volume</u> of wood in the pencil?

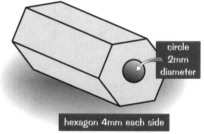

circle
2mm
diameter

hexagon 4mm each side

3cm

Spine radius
1.5cm

12cm

Q3 In a set of encyclopedias, each book can be thought of in cross-section as a rectangle with a semi circular spine radius 1.5 cm.
If each leather bound book in the set was 20 cm high, 12 cm wide and 3 cm deep, <u>how many</u> encyclopaedia can be fitted upon a 1 m long shelf?

Q4 A tree trunk can be thought of as a circular prism with a height of 1.7 m.
If the trunk has radius 60 cm what <u>volume of wood</u> is this in m³?

Q5 A cylindrical copper pipe has insulation in the form of a foam tube placed around the outside of it. The pipe has external dimensions of 10 cm diameter and 10 m length. The foam tubing is 25 mm thick.

   a) Find the <u>cross-sectional area</u> of the pipe.

   b) Find the <u>cross-sectional area</u> of insulation.

   c) Find the <u>volume</u> of the insulation over the 10 m length.

Questions on Pie Charts

When constructing a pie chart, follow the three steps:

1) Add up the numbers in each sector to get the <u>TOTAL</u>.
2) Divide 360° by the <u>TOTAL</u> to get the <u>MULTIPLIER</u>.
3) Multiply <u>EVERY</u> number by the <u>MULTIPLIER</u> to get the <u>ANGLE</u> of each <u>SEGMENT</u>.

Q1   <u>Construct a pie chart</u>, using the template on the right, to show the following data:

Type of washing powder	Households on one estate using it
Swash	22
Sudso	17
Bubblefoam	18
Cleanyo	21
Wundersuds	12

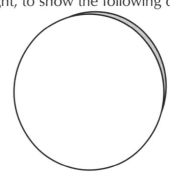

Q2   In the year 1998/99, 380,000 students studied IT in Scotland. The <u>distribution</u> of students for the <u>whole of Britain</u> is shown in the pie chart.
Use a <u>protractor</u> on the diagram to find the number of students studying IT in each of the other parts of the U.K. (rounded to the nearest 10,000).

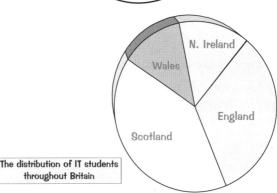

The distribution of IT students throughout Britain

Q3   The pie chart shows the results of a survey of forty 11 year olds when asked what their

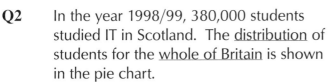

<u>favourite vegetable</u> is with Sunday lunch. Which one of the following may be <u>deduced</u> from the information in the <u>pie chart</u>?

a) Potatoes are the <u>least popular</u> vegetable.
b) 3/4 of the children <u>like potatoes</u> of some type.
c) 1/10 of the children like <u>carrots or cauliflower</u>.
d) 11/40 of the children asked what their favourite vegetable is, replied "<u>Don't eat vegetables</u>."

Q4   Mr and Mrs Tight think they have the family <u>budget</u> under control.
Mr and Mrs Spendthrift try to argue with Mr and Mrs Tight that they too can control their spending.
They produce <u>two pie charts</u> to represent their spending habits.
Give <u>2 reasons</u> why these pie charts are <u>unhelpful</u>.

Questions on Graphs and Charts

Q1 Having seen the <u>line graph</u> opposite, a Quality Control Manager said "Admittedly we do have some complaints about our products, but from July complaints have tailed off, so our products must be of a better quality." From the graph, do you think this statement is <u>correct</u>? Why/Why not?

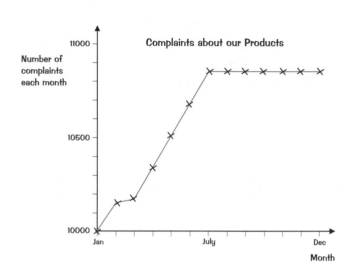

Q2 Draw a typical <u>scatter graph</u> that you think would be associated with each of the pair of variables below. Say in each case what type of correlation you are intending to show, and label the axes with the variables.

a) Ice cream sales and temperature.

b) Umbrellas sold and rainfall.

c) Caravan prices and age of caravans.

d) Number of motorcyclists on the road and the number of PC's sold.

Q3 The table contains the mean monthly temperatures for Leaningdale, a hamlet in Cumbria, and the rainfall/snowfall for each month.

Month	J	F	M	A	M	J	J	A	S	O	N	D
Temperature (°C)	2	1	3	6	8	12	16	18	19	11	9	2
Rainfall/snowfall (mm)	30	34	20	24	15	10	13	15	11	11	26	32

a) Draw a <u>scatter diagram</u> to see if a correlation exists between <u>temperature</u> and <u>rainfall/snowfall</u> in the hamlet of Leaningdale.

b) Put on your diagram a <u>line of best fit</u>. Give a sentence describing the type of correlation you see.

Q4 List the values shown in this stem and leaf diagram in ascending order.

Just to start you off, the first five values are: 3, 3, 3, 5, 8.

```
0 | 3 3 3 5 8 8 9
1 | 2 3 4 4 8 8 9
2 | 0 2 2 4
3 | 1 3
```

Key: 1 | 4 means 14

Q5 Draw a stem and leaf diagram to represent the data below. Include a key.

101, 115, 122, 132, 126, 102, 124, 141, 139, 128, 123, 119, 131, 120, 125, 123, 117, 114, 130, 127

Questions on Averages and Range

If you don't learn these 4 basic definitions, you'll miss out on some of the easiest marks. Have a go at the questions on the next few pages and you'll see what I mean.

The 4 basic definitions:	
1) <u>Mode</u>	Most <u>Common</u>
2) <u>Median</u>	<u>Middle</u> Value
3) <u>Mean</u>	<u>Average</u> (Total of Items ÷ Number of Items)
4) <u>Range</u>	<u>Difference</u> between the <u>Smallest</u> and the <u>Biggest</u>

Q1 Metre rulers are made by a machine. Accurate measurements with a micrometer show that they lie between 99 cm and 101cm. A <u>sample of 20</u> gave the following readings:

101.0	100.5	99.4	100.2	100.6	100.0	100.6	100.7	100.9	99.8
99.7	99.3	99.7	100.1	100.0	99.7	99.5	99.6	100.7	100.9

a) What is the <u>mean</u> length?
b) What is the <u>modal</u> length?
c) What is the <u>median</u> length?

The mean involves a bit more calculation, but hey, you are doing maths.

Q2 Find the mode and median <u>shoe size</u> of the 30 school children whose shoe sizes are:

4	2	3	4	4	5	4	2	4	3
2	1	3	1	3	2	5	3	2	3
3	2	3	2	4	6	7	2	3	1

Q3 Find the <u>mean age</u> of eight children whose ages are:

13 years 6 months   13 years 8 months   13 years 4 months   13 years
13 years 1 month   12 years 10 months   12 years 9 months   12 years 6 months

Q4 Find the median of 8, 6, 6, 3, 2 and 1.

Q5 Find the mode of 10, 9, 8, 8, 8, 8, 7, 7, 4 and 3.

Just identify the most frequent value and the middle value — easy.

Q6 A firm sending out catalogues throughout the country posted <u>88 catalogues</u> first class on <u>Monday</u>. The clients received them over the week: <u>40</u> on <u>Tuesday</u>, <u>28</u> on <u>Wednesday</u>, <u>9</u> on <u>Thursday</u>, <u>6</u> on <u>Friday</u> and the <u>remainder</u> on <u>Saturday</u>.

a) Find the modal number of days necessary for the catalogues to arrive.
b) Find the median number of days necessary for the catalogues to arrive.
c) "The <u>majority</u> of first class post arrives <u>within 2 days</u>."
   Is the above statement <u>true</u> or <u>false</u> in the light of the data?

Q7 Find the median, mode, mean and range of the following data:
a) 20, 18, 16, 14, 12, 16, 0, 4, 6, 8
b) 5, 1, 2, 2, 4, 3, 3, 4, 3

Q8 a) Give two advantages and one disadvantage of using the mean.
b) Give two advantages and one disadvantage of using the mode.
c) Give three advantages and disadvantages of using the median.

Questions on Frequency Tables

Frequency Tables look quite tricky, so you'd better
make sure you know how they work.

Frequency Tables contain three rows:

1) The 1st row (or column) gives us the Group Labels,
   eg weights of 50 kg, 55 kg, etc.
2) The 2nd row (or column) is the actual frequency data,
   eg 10 people weigh 50 kg, etc.
3) The 3rd row (or column) is just the other two multiplied
   together and is left for you to fill in.

Q1 120 male pupils were weighed to the
nearest kg. Calculate:
a) the median weight
b) the modal weight
c) the mean weight, by first completing
the table.

Mass (kg)	Frequency	Mass x Freq.
61	22	
62	44	
63	35	
64	19	

Q2 100 female pupils were weighed to the
nearest kg. Calculate:
a) the median weight
b) the mode
c) the mean by completing the table

Mass	49	50	51	52
Frequency	20	35	25	20

Q3 The pages of my text book are <u>numbered</u> from
<u>1 to 300</u>. Complete the table showing the
frequencies of pages whose numbers have <u>1, 2
and 3 digits</u>.
a) State <u>directly</u> the mode.
b) Find the median
c) Find the mean. Does it <u>make sense</u> to have this value? Why / why not?

No. of digits	1	2	3
Frequency			

Q4 The Samaritans log all calls to their helpline. The number of <u>calls per day</u> received by their
helpline over a given <u>year</u> are shown below. Find the median and mode.

No. of calls	10	11	12	13	14	15	16 and over
No. of days	137	104	56	31	18	13	6

Q5 20 pupils are asked to estimate the length, to the nearest cm, of their teacher's table. Put
the estimates in the <u>frequency table</u> below:

148 142 140 138 136 136 132 128 126 128
146 144 138 140 138 134 138 128 124 124

Estimate	124	126	128	132	134	136	138	140	142	144	146	148
Frequency												

a) Find the mode.   b) Find the median.   c) State the range.

Questions on Frequency Tables

Q6 Using the computerised till in a shoe shop, the manager can predict what stock to order from the previous week's sales. Below is the tabulated print out for <u>last week</u> for <u>men's shoes</u>.

Shoe size	5	6	7	8	9	10	11
frequency	9	28	56	70	56	28	9

a) The mean, mode and median for this data can be compared. For each of the following statements decide whether it <u>could be true</u> or is <u>definitely false</u>?
i) The <u>mode</u> for this data is <u>70</u>.
ii) The <u>mean</u> is <u>greater than</u> the <u>median</u> for this distribution.
iii) The mean, median and mode are <u>all equal</u> in this distribution.

b) What <u>percentage</u> of customers bought shoes of the <u>mean size</u> from last weeks sales data?
i) 30% **ii)** 70% **iii)** 0.273% or **iv)** 27.3% ?

Q7 'White Ridge Back' sows can give birth to a number of piglets between 5 and 10 inclusive.

From the table:
a) state the mode
b) state the median
c) find the mean.

Number of piglets born	5	6	7	8	9	10
frequency	3	4	5	4	7	2

If a farmer wishes to promote the 'White Ridge Back' sow as the <u>most prolific breeder</u>, then which of the three 'averages' would he <u>not include</u> in his advert in 'Bacon & Ham' weekly?

Q8 Blackshire County Libraries store data on borrowers who they lend books to. The figures in the table show books

Number of books lent to a person over six months	<10	11	12	13	14	15	16	17
Frequency	20	32	38	40	70	28	14	6

lent over a six month period. Find the <u>mean number of books</u> lent <u>per person</u> for the six month period. Give an approximate, <u>sensible</u> value for this.

Q9 The <u>total</u> weight of 15 rugby players is 1350 kg.
The <u>total</u> weight of 9 ballet dancers is 360 kg.
What is the <u>mean</u> weight of the <u>group</u> of 24 people when put together?

Q10 A survey of the number of <u>occupants</u> in cars arriving at Blugdon High, shows that the mean number of occupants is 2. Unfortunately, just after carrying out the survey a raindrop obliterated the number of cars with <u>3</u> occupants. Find out how

Number of occupants	0	1	2	3	4
Number of cars	0	27	15		0

many cars had <u>exactly 3 occupants</u> by using the legible data.

Questions on Grouped Frequency Tables

As a rule these are trickier than standard frequency tables — you'll certainly have to tread carefully here. Have a good look at the box below and make sure you remember it.

Class Boundaries and Mid-Interval Values

1) The <u>CLASS BOUNDARIES</u> are the precise values where you go from one group to the next.
2) The <u>MID-INTERVAL VALUES</u> are just what they sound like — the middle of the group.

shoe size	1 - 2	3 - 4	5 - 6	7 - 8
frequency	15	10	3	1

The Mid-Interval Values are 1.5, 3.5, 5.5, etc.
The Class Boundaries are 2.5, 4.5, 6.5, etc.

Q1 In a survey of test results in a French class at Blugdon High, these grades were achieved by the 23 pupils.

Identify:
a) the Class Boundaries between the groups
b) the Mid-Interval Values for each of the groups.

(grade) score	(E) 31-40	(D) 41-50	(C) 51-60	(B) 61-70
frequency	4	7	8	4

$$\text{Mean} = \frac{\text{Overall Total (Frequency} \times \text{Mid} - \text{Interval Value)}}{\text{Frequency Total}}$$

Q2 This table shows times for each team of swimmers, the Dolphins and the Sharks. Complete the table then use the mid-interval technique to estimate the mean time for each team.

Dolphins			Sharks		
Time interval (seconds)	Frequency	Mid-interval value	Time interval (seconds)	Frequency	Mid-interval value
14-19	3	16.5	14-19	6	16.5
20-25	7	22.5	20-25	15	22.5
26-31	15		26-31	33	
32-37	32		32-37	59	
38-43	45		38-43	20	
44-49	30		44-49	8	
50-55	5		50-55	2	

Q3 Complete the table below by filling in the cumulative frequency.

Sponsored Walk Donations	1p - 10p	11p - 20p	21p - 30p	31p - 40p	41p - 50p
Frequency	10	13	16	15	12
Cumulative Frequency	10	23			

Cumulative frequency just means a running total of the frequency data.

Questions on the Cumulative Frequency Curve

 Ah, curves, that's more like it. From cumulative frequency curves you get **three things**. Look at this box and make sure you know what to do.

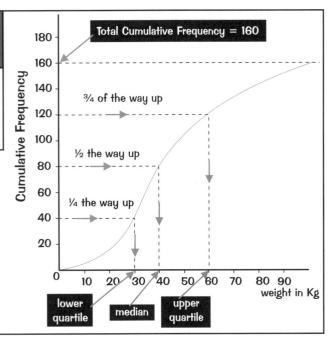

From the Cumulative Frequency Curve you can get 3 vital statistics:

1) <u>MEDIAN</u>
2) <u>LOWER / UPPER QUARTILES</u>
3) <u>INTERQUARTILE RANGE</u>

From the graph:
MEDIAN = 40 kg
LOWER QUARTILE = 30 kg
UPPER QUARTILE = 60 kg
INTER-QUARTILE RANGE = 60 kg–30 kg
= 30 kg

Q1 This table shows the number of bowlers, out of a total of 80, who took the wickets in cricket matches over the course of a season.

a) Draw a cumulative frequency diagram from this data.

No. of Wickets	1 - 10	11 - 20	21 - 30	31 - 40	41 - 50	51 - 60	61 - 70	71 - 80	81 - 90	91 - 100
No. of Bowlers	2	3	5	7	19	16	14	10	3	1
Cumulative Freq.										

b) Use it to estimate the median.

c) What is the interquartile range of the data?

Q2 The lengths of 25 snakes are measured to the nearest cm, and then grouped in a frequency table. Which of the following sentences may be true and which have to be false?

a) The median length is 161cm.

b) The range is 20 cm.

c) The modal class has 7 snakes.

d) The median length is 158cm.

Length	151 - 155	156 - 160	161 -165	166 - 170	171 - 175	Total
frequency	4	8	7	5	1	25

Q3 This table shows the frequency distribution for 70 candidates taking a Christmas Mock Exam.
Draw a cumulative frequency curve and use it to estimate:

a) the median

b) the Upper and Lower quartiles

c) the Interquartile Range.

Class interval	Frequency	Cumulative Frequency
45-49	1	
50-54	0	
55-59	3	
60-64	6	
65-69	11	
70-74	18	
75-79	16	
80-84	9	
85-89	5	
90-94	1	
95-99	0	

 I know that "interquartile range" sounds a bit of a ridiculous name, but it's actually not a bad description — it's the difference between the quartiles. Remember to take your reading from the bottom scale — take it from anywhere else and you've blown it.

Questions on Box Plots

Well, as they say, there's no box plots without cumulative frequency curves...

To draw a box plot:

1) Use the same scale as the c.f. curve.

2) Draw lines down from the median, upper and lower quartiles and maximum and minimum lines.

3) Draw a box between the upper and lower quartiles, and divide it in two by drawing a line down the box for the median. Then finish it off with horizontal lines (or "whiskers") from the box to the maximum/minimum points.

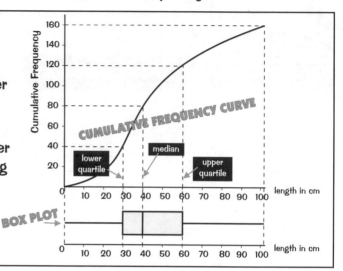

Q1   Egbert noted the attention span of several of his friends, while talking to them about the fall of communism in Eastern Europe. The results, in seconds, were as follows:

33	23	31	33	37	42	27	42	36	34
30	25	43	39	38	49	33	38	47	36
21	31	28	34	31	36	30	39	32	33

a) Put the data into this frequency table.

Attention Span (seconds)	20 – 24	25 – 29	30 – 34	35 – 39	40 – 44	45 – 49
Frequency						
Cumulative Frequency						

b) Construct the cumulative frequency curve.

c) Draw the box plot underneath the cumulative frequency curve.

Q2   The 100 scores in a TV gameshow are presented in the table below.

Score	31 – 40	41 – 50	51 – 60	61 – 70	71 – 80	81 – 90	91 – 100
Frequency	4	12	21	32	19	8	4
Cumulative Frequency							

a) Complete the table.

b) Plot the cumulative frequency curve.

c) Draw the box plot.

Complete this phrase:
"I wandered lonely as a..."

A: penguin   C: poet
B: cloud   D: fish

Questions on Powers (Indices)

Hang on there. Before you try this page, make sure you know the eight rules for powers — you'll find them on P.71 of The Revision Guide.

The small number is called the <u>power</u> or <u>index number</u>. Remember the plural of index is <u>indices</u>.

$5^4 = 5 \times 5 \times 5 \times 5 =$ _____

we say "five to the power four"

$8^3 = 8 \times 8 \times 8 =$ _____

we say "eight to the power three" or "eight cubed"

To save time try using the power button on your calculator

eg.

Q1   Complete the following:
a) $2^4 = 2 \times 2 \times 2 \times 2 =$
b) $10^3 = 10 \times 10 \times 10 =$
c) $3^5 = 3 \times ...$ =
d) $4^6 = 4 \times$ =
e) $1^9 = 1 \times$ =
f) $5^6 = 5 \times$ =

Q2   Simplify the following:
a) $2 \times 2 \times 2 \times 2 \times 2 \times 2 \times 2 \times 2$
b) $12 \times 12 \times 12 \times 12 \times 12$
c) $x \times x \times x \times x \times x \times x \times x \times x$
d) $m \times m \times m$
e) $y \times y \times y \times y$
f) $z \times z \times z \times z \times z \times z$

Q3   Complete the following (the first one has been done for you):
a) $10^2 \times 10^3 = (10 \times 10) \times (10 \times 10 \times 10)$ $= 10^5$
b) $10^3 \times 10^4 =$ =
c) $10^4 \times 10^2 =$ =
d) $10^5 \times 10^3 =$ =
e) What is the <u>quick method</u> for writing down the final result in **b)**, **c)** and **d)**?

Easy — you'll have learnt this from your eight rules of powers.

Q4   Complete (the first one has been done for you):

a) $2^4 \div 2^2 = \dfrac{(2 \times 2 \times 2 \times 2)}{(2 \times 2)} = 2^2$

c) $4^5 \div 4^3 = \dfrac{(4 \times 4 \times 4 \times 4 \times 4)}{} =$

b) $2^5 \div 2^2 = \dfrac{(2 \times 2 \times 2 \times 2 \times 2)}{(2 \times 2)} =$

d) $8^5 \div 8^2 =$ =

e) What is the quick method for writing down the final result in **b)**, **c)** and **d)**?

Q5   Which of the following are <u>true</u>?

a) $2^4 \times 2^6 = 2^{10}$
b) $2^2 \times 2^3 \times 2^4 = 2^9$
c) $2^3 \times 2^2 = 2^6$
d) $4^{10} \times 4^4 \times 4^2 = 4^{18}$
e) $2^1 \times 2^3 \times 2^4 = 2^8$
f) $10^4 \times 10^2 = 10^8$
g) $2^{20} \div 2^5 = 2^4$
h) $3^{12} \div 3^4 = 3^8$
i) $4^6 \div 6^4 = 4^2$
j) $10^{20} \div 10^3 = 10^{17}$
k) $4^6 \div (4^2 \times 4^3) = 4^1$
l) $9^2 \times (9^{30} \div 9^{25}) = 9^{10}$

Q6   Write each of the following as a <u>single term</u>:
a) $10^6 \div 10^4$
b) $(8^2 \times 8^5) \div 8^3$
c) $6^{10} \div (6^2 \times 6^3)$
d) $x^2 \times x^3$
e) $a^5 \times a^4$
f) $p^4 \times p^5 \times p^6$
g) $x^3 \div x^2$
h) $a^5 \div a^3$
i) $h^{12} \div (h^4 \times h^4)$

Questions on Powers (Indices)

Grab your calculator for this bit — you'd better get used to that powers button ...

Q7 Use your <u>calculator</u> to find the exact value of

a) 4^3 c) 10^4 e) 12^5 g) 13^3 i) 1^{28}

b) 3^5 d) 4^1 f) 15^3 h) 1^{10} j) 5^8

Q8 Use your calculator to find the exact value of

a) 5^{-1} c) 50^{-1} e) 10^{-5} g) 4^{-2}

b) 10^{-2} d) 2^{-3} f) 100^{-1} h) 1^{-5}

Have another go at Q8, and don't go to Q9 until you've got the same answers twice — go on, it won't take you long.

Q9 Write as a <u>single power</u>:

a) $2^4 \times 2^3$ e) $8^3 \div 8^1$ i) $x^4 \div x^{-1}$ m) $3^{-2} \times (3^{-4} \div 3^0)$

b) $2^6 \times 2^0$ f) $4^6 \div 4^{-2}$ j) $y^3 \div y^2$ n) $(3^{-2})^3$

c) $4^2 \times 4^{-2}$ g) $7^{-3} \div 7^{-4}$ k) $y^4 \times y^4$ o) $(x^2)^3$

d) $4^6 \times 4^3$ h) $8^{10} \div 8^{-2}$ l) $m^4 \times m^{-2}$ p) $(4^{-1})^4$

Q10 Write as a <u>single power</u>:

a) $(x^2)^4$ b) $(y^6)^2$ c) $(z^{10})^2$ d) $(x^2)^{-3}$ e) $(y^{-1})^6$

Q11 Find the <u>value of n</u> where $12^5 \div 12^n = 12^7$

Remember your powers rule for dividing — you simply do this one backwards.

Q12 Find the <u>reciprocal</u> of 1000 and express as a power of 10.

Q13 Remove the brackets from the following and express as a single power:

a) $(3^4 \times 3^2) \div (3^6 \times 3^3)$ d) $(3^6)^{-2}$

b) $(4^{10} \times 4^{12}) \times 4^3$ e) $4^2 \times 4^{-1} \times 4^6 \times (4^2 \div 4^3)$

c) $10^2 \div (10^3 \times 10^{12})$ f) $(5^2 \times 5^3) \div (5^6 \div 5^4)$

Questions on Growth and Decay

Hey look — it's another of those "there is only one formula to learn and you use it for every question" topics.

So I reckon you'd better learn **The Formula** then...

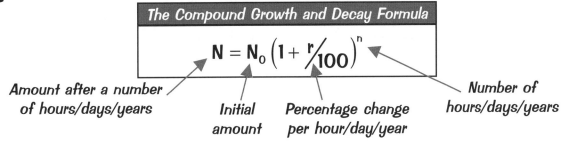

The Compound Growth and Decay Formula

$$N = N_0 \left(1 + \frac{r}{100}\right)^n$$

Amount after a number of hours/days/years

Initial amount

Percentage change per hour/day/year

Number of hours/days/years

Q1 Calculate the amount in each account if:
   a) £200 is invested for 10 yrs at 9% compound interest per annum
   b) £500 is invested for 3 yrs at 7% compound interest per annum
   c) £750 is invested for 30 months at 8% compound interest per annum
   d) £1000 is invested for 15 months at 6.5% compound interest per annum.

Q2 A colony of bacteria grows at the compound rate of 12% per hour. Initially there are 200 bacteria.
   a) How many will there be after 3 hours?
   b) How many will there be after 1 day?

Just make sure you get the increase and decrease the right way round... basically, just check your answer sounds like you'd expect — and if it doesn't, do it again.

Q3 A radioactive element was observed every day and the mass remaining was measured. Initially there was 9 kg but this decreased at the compound rate of 3% per day. How much radioactive element will be left after:
   a) 3 days
   b) 6 days
   c) 1 week
   d) 4 weeks?
   Give your answer to 3 d.p.

Q4 Money is invested on the stock market. During a recession the value of the shares falls by 2% per week.
   Find the value of the stock if:
   a) £2000 was invested for a fortnight
   b) £30,000 was invested for a month
   c) £500 was invested for 7 weeks
   d) £100,000 was invested for a year.

I'd go for Victorian rolling pins, myself...

Questions on Simultaneous Equations

The name makes it sound scary, but these are just 2 equations with the same solutions.

Q1 By substituting x = 3 and y = 4 into the following equations, show that these values are solutions to the equations: 4x + y = 16   2x – y = 2.

Q2 Show by substitution that x = 4 and y = –2, are the solutions to both these equations:
3x – 4y = 20   5x + 2y =16.

Q3 Show by substitution that x = –5 and y = 0, are the solutions to both these equations:
3y – 2x = 10   3x + 2y = -15

Q4 Given that x and y satisfy the following equations, find the value of y when x = 4:
2x – y = 8   3x – 4y = 12

Q5 Given that x and y satisfy the following equations, find the value of x when y = 3:
3x + 4y = 24   5x – 5y = 5

Q6 Given that x and y satisfy the following equations, find the value of y when x = -2:
5y – 3x = 16   4y + x = 6

To solve simultaneous equations from scratch, you've got to get rid of either x or y first — to leave you with an equation with just one unknown in it. You do this by adding or subtracting equations — have a look at this example:

Eg: solve the simultaneous equations 2x + 3y = 13 and 2x – y = 1.

1) There is a <u>2x</u> in both equations, so <u>eliminate x</u> by <u>subtracting</u> one equation from the other: (2x – 2x) + (3y – -y) = (13 – 1), so   4y = 12   hence   y = 3

2) Then <u>substitute</u> y = 3 back into either equation, to find x: 2x + 9 = 13
2x = 13 – 9 = 4 hence   x = 2

Q7 Use the above example as a guide to solve the following:

a) 3x + y = 7
2x - y = 3

b) x + y = 12
x – y = 2

c) x + 3y = 10
x – y = –2

d) 5x + 2y = 3
2x – 2y = 4

e) 4x – y = 13
2x – y = 5

f) 8x + 3y = 8
5x – 3y = 5

g) x + 3y = 10
2x – 3y = 2

h) 8x + 6y = 2
2x – 6y = 3

i) x – 12y = 16
5x + 12y = 8

j) 10x – 2y = –8
10x + y = 19

k) 11x + 3y = 5
7x – 3y = 13

l) 2x + 7y = 11
2x + 3y = 7

m) x + 8y = 7
4x + 8y = 4

n) 5x – 3y = –2
–5x + y = 4

Q8 Rearrange <u>one</u> of the equations <u>before</u> eliminating either the x term or y term by adding or subtracting the pair of equations, then solve:

a) 3y – 4x = 10
4x – 2y = –8

b) 3x + y = 13
2y – 3x = 8

c) 3y + 4x = 10
4x – 2y = –8

d) y + 1 = 3x
y – x = 3

e) y + x = 2
y – ½x + 1 = 0

f) y – 3 = 2x
y = x - 1

g) 4y – 3x = 22
3x – 2y = –14

h) y = 5 – 2x
y = x – 4

i) 2y + x = 2
y + x + 1 = 0

j) 3y + 2x = 19
2x + y = 1

k) 9x - y = 12
4y - 9x = 6

l) 6x + 2y = 5
3y - 6x = 15

Questions on Simultaneous Equations

Multiply one equation by a number before adding or subtracting. Solve the equations.

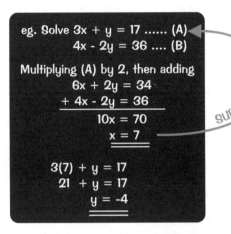

eg. Solve $3x + y = 17$ ...... (A)
$4x - 2y = 36$ .... (B)

Multiplying (A) by 2, then adding
$6x + 2y = 34$
$+ 4x - 2y = 36$
$\overline{10x = 70}$
$x = 7$

$3(7) + y = 17$
$21 + y = 17$
$y = -4$

SUB INTO (A)

Remember
When you multiply an equation by **2**
<u>every</u> term in that equation doubles.
When you multiply an equation by **3**
<u>every</u> term in that equation trebles.

Remember
Always substitute your first answer back into
an <u>original</u> equation to find the second answer.
There is less chance of making a mistake this way.

Each time you do a step, <u>write it down</u> — "Multiply A by 2" — that
sort of thing. I know it sounds a waste of time, but if you hash things
up, it'll be easier to check what went wrong.

Q9 Find x and y in the following:

a) $3x + 2y = 12$
$2x + y = 7$

b) $5x - y = 17$
$2x + 3y = 0$

c) $x + 3y = 11$
$2x + 5y = 19$

d) $5x + 3y = 24$
$x + 5y = -4$

e) $3x + 2y = 3$
$2x + y = 23$

f) $4x + 2y = 8$
$x + 3y = 2$

g) $x + 14y = -2$
$2x + 3y = 21$

h) $3x + 2y = 21$
$2x - y = 7$

i) $6x - y = -4$
$3x - 2y = 1$

j) $5x - 4y = 7$
$7x - 2y = 17$

k) $8x - y = 6$
$7x + 5y = 17$

l) $8x + 3y = 27$
$2x - 5y = 1$

Q10 Multiply <u>both</u> equations by a number before adding or subtracting. Solve the equations:

a) $3x + 2y = 13$
$2x + 3y = 7$

b) $4x + 2y = 10$
$7x + 3y = 16$

c) $2x + 3y = 16$
$3x + 2y = 9$

d) $6x - 3y = 3$
$5x - 2y = 4$

e) $7x - 3y = 18$
$5x + 2y = 17$

f) $11x - 3y = 8$
$9x + 4y = 13$

g) $7y - 3x = 2$
$5y - 2x = 2$

h) $5x - 8y = 12$
$4x - 7y = 9$

i) $4x - 2y = -6$
$5x + 3y = 20$

j) $7x + 5y = 66$
$3x - 4y = 16$

k) $10x + 4y = 2$
$8x + 3y = 1$

l) $3x + 4y = 19$
$4x - 3y = -8$

The next few questions are a bit of a mixed bag — there's some rearranging,
some multiplying and some plain and simple adding or subtracting. Enjoy.

Q11 Solve the following <u>simultaneous</u> equations:

a) $4x - y = 5$
$2x + y = -2$

b) $5x - 4 = 4y$
$2y + 2 = x$

c) $4x - 3y = 15$
$2x + 3y = 3$

d) $3x + 8y = 24$
$x + y = 3$

e) $3y - 8x = 24$
$3y + 2x = 9$

f) $y = 13 - 4x$
$3x + 2y = 16$

g) $2x - 3y = 1$
$11y - 7x = 5$

h) $y + 1 = 2x$
$y = x + 2$

Questions on Simultaneous Equations

It's DIY time — you've got to write your own equations, and then solve them. Not asking for much...

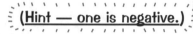

Q12 Two numbers x and y have a <u>sum</u> of 15 and a <u>difference</u> of 3.
   a) Write a pair of simultaneous equations in x and y.
   b) Solve for x and y.

Q13 Two numbers x and y have a sum of 4 and a difference of 12
Find the values of x and y.   **(Hint — one is negative.)**

Q14 A farmer has a choice of buying 6 sheep and 5 pigs for £430 <u>or</u> 4 sheep and 10 pigs for £500 at auction.
   a) If sheep cost £x and pigs cost £y, write down his <u>two choices</u> as a pair of simultaneous equations.
   b) Solve for x and y.

Q15 Six apples and four oranges cost £1.90, whereas eight apples and two oranges cost £1.80. Find the cost of an apple and the cost of an orange.

Q16 Find the value of x and y for each of the following rectangles, by first writing down a pair of simultaneous equations and then solving them.

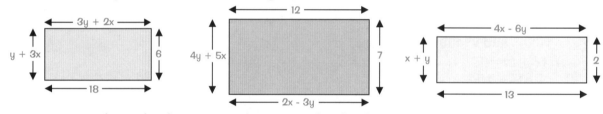

Q17 Two groups of people place two orders in a café. The first group orders 4 cups of coffee and 2 cups of tea and their bill is for £4.80. The second group orders 3 cups of coffee and 5 cups of tea and their bill is for £6.05.
   a) Write down two simultaneous equations involving a cup of coffee (c) and a cup of tea (t).
   b) Find the value of c and t, <u>in pence</u>.

Q18 A box has length (x + y) cm, height (y + 4) cm and width 2x cm, where the length is 12 cm and the height is 11 cm.
   a) Write down a pair of simultaneous equations involving x and y.
   b) Solve the simultaneous equations to find the value of x and y.
   c) By substituting in your value of x, find the <u>volume</u> of the cube in cm³.

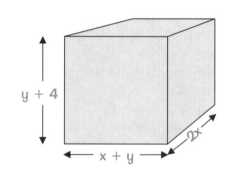

Q19

Two customers enter a shop to buy milk and corn flakes. Mrs Smith buys 5 pints of milk and 2 boxes of corn flakes and spends £3.44. Mr Brown buys 4 pints of milk and 3 boxes of corn flakes and receives £6.03 <u>change</u> after paying with a £10 note.
Write down a pair of simultaneous equations and solve them to find the price in pence of a pint of milk (m) and a box of cornflakes (c).

Questions on Simultaneous Eq' Graphs

The solution of two simultaneous equations is simply the X and Y values where their graphs cross

1) Simultaneous equations can be plotted as two <u>straight-line graphs</u> on the <u>same axes</u>.
2) The point where the lines cross will have <u>coordinates</u> equal to the <u>values of x and y</u> which satisfy both equations.

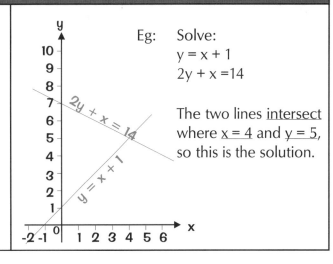

Eg: Solve:
$y = x + 1$
$2y + x = 14$

The two lines <u>intersect</u> where <u>x = 4</u> and <u>y = 5</u>, so this is the solution.

Q1 Solve these simultaneous equations by looking at the graphs. Then check your answers by substituting the values back into the equations.

a) $y + 2x = 9$
$3y = x + 6$

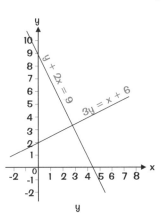

d) $y = x + 6$
$3y + x = 18$

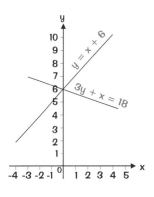

b) $y = 2x + 14$
$2y = 8 - x$

e) $y + x = 1$
$3y = x + 11$

c) $x + y = 6$
$3y = x + 6$

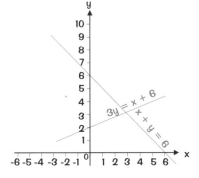

f) $y = 2x - 13$
$2y + x + 6 = 0$

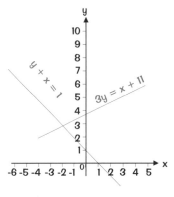

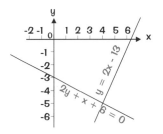

STAGE THREE

Questions on Quadratics

It's factorising Jim, but not as we know it... Better watch out with these, I reckon.

Factorising Quadratics

1) A <u>QUADRATIC</u> expression is of the form $[x^2 + bx + c]$
2) <u>FACTORISING</u> a quadratic expression means putting it into two brackets.

Eg: Factorising $x^2 - 2x - 8$
will give $(x - 4)(x + 2)$.

To check this works,
multiply out again:
$(x - 4)(x + 2) = x^2 + 2x - 4x - 8$
$= x^2 - 2x - 8$

$-8 = -1 \times 8$
-8×1
-2×4
-4×2

$(x \quad)(x \quad)$

To complete the brackets find two numbers
which multiply to give c, and <u>at the same time</u>
either + or - to give b. Finally put in +or - signs,
checking that the two brackets will multiply out
to give the equation.

Q1 Factorise the following equations:

a) $x^2 + 3x + 2$
b) $x^2 + 5x + 6$
c) $x^2 + 8x + 15$

d) $x^2 + 7x + 10$
e) $x^2 + 12x + 27$
f) $x^2 + 15x + 36$

g) $x^2 + 10x + 24$
h) $x^2 + 11x + 24$
i) $x^2 + 12x + 36$

 Your best bet with Q1 is the old guessing game.
Come up with a pair of numbers, then try adding and multiplying them.

Remember, they've got to multiply together to make the number at the
end and add together to make the x term in the middle.

Q2 Factorise each of the following:

a) $x^2 + 3x$
b) $x^2 + 8x$
c) $x^2 + 10x$

d) $x^2 - 4x$
e) $x^2 - 8x$
f) $x^2 - 20x$

g) $2x - x^2$
h) $5x - x^2$
i) $9x - x^2$

Q2 is a bit like the ones from P.18. These are quadratics,
though, but you can still factorise them in the same way.

Q3 Factorise the following:

a) $x^2 + x - 6$
b) $x^2 - x - 12$
c) $x^2 - 2x - 35$
d) $x^2 - 4x - 32$

e) $x^2 - 3x - 54$
f) $x^2 - 5x + 6$
g) $x^2 - 6x + 8$
h) $x^2 - 11x + 30$

i) $x^2 - 13x + 30$
j) $x^2 - 11x + 28$
k) $x^2 - 3x - 40$
l) $x^2 + 10x - 24$

Q4 Factorise the following using the difference of two squares:

a) $x^2 - 9$
b) $x^2 - 64$

c) $4x^2 - 36$
d) $9x^2 - 100$

e) $x^2 - y^2$
f) $16x^2 - 25y^2$

 I've seen the sign... when you get any negative numbers in there, look at where
the signs are and think about your sign rules for multiplying — it'll help you work
out the signs of the numbers you're looking for. Which is bound to save time.

Q5 Factorise the <u>quadratic expression</u> $x^2 + 90x - 1000$.

Questions on Quadratics

We're solving them now — but it's OK, it's only an (easy) step on from factorising.

Solving Quadratic Equations

1) A <u>QUADRATIC EQUATION</u> is usually of the form $[x^2 + bx + c = 0]$
2) It can be factorised to give $(x \pm ?)(x \pm ?) = 0$
3) To find the <u>two</u> answers <u>either</u> the <u>first</u> bracket must equal zero, <u>or</u> the <u>second</u> bracket must <u>equal zero</u>.

Eg: Solve $x^2 - 4x = 21$
$x^2 - 4x - 21 = 0$
$(x - 7)(x + 3) = 0$
<u>$x=7$</u> or <u>$x=-3$</u>

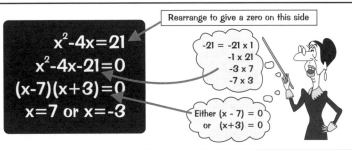

Rearrange to give a zero on this side

$x^2 - 4x = 21$
$x^2 - 4x - 21 = 0$
$(x-7)(x+3) = 0$
$x = 7$ or $x = -3$

$-21 = -21 \times 1$
-1×21
-3×7
-7×3

Either $(x - 7) = 0$
or $(x + 3) = 0$

Q6 Solve the following quadratic equations:

a) $(x + 4)(x - 3) = 0$
b) $(x + 2)(x + 8) = 0$
c) $(x - 1)(x - 7) = 0$
d) $(x + 4)(x + 18) = 0$
e) $(x - 3)(x - 11) = 0$
f) $(x - 2)^2 = 0$
g) $(x + 3)^2 = 0$
h) $(x - 9)^2 = 0$

i) $(x + 4)^2 = 0$
j) $(x - 25)^2 = 0$
k) $x(x + 4) = 0$
l) $x(x - 7) = 0$
m) $x(x + 30) = 0$
n) $x(x + 2) = 0$
o) $(3 - x)(4 - x) = 0$

For the ones where you get one bracket squared, eg $(x+1)^2 = 0$, there's only the one answer (Which is x=-1, in this case).

Q7 Find x by solving the following quadratic equations:

a) $x^2 + 6x + 8 = 0$
b) $x^2 + 3x - 10 = 0$
c) $x^2 + 10x + 25 = 0$
d) $x^2 - 5x + 6 = 0$
e) $x^2 - 6x + 9 = 0$

f) $x^2 - 2x + 1 = 0$
g) $x^2 - 3x - 18 = 0$
h) $x^2 - 4x + 3 = 0$
i) $x^2 - 7x + 10 = 0$
j) $x^2 - x - 20 = 0$

k) $x^2 - 4x - 5 = 0$
l) $x^2 + 9x + 8 = 0$
m) $x^2 + 6x - 7 = 0$
n) $x^2 + x - 12 = 0$
o) $x^2 + 14x + 49 = 0$

(Don't forget you've got to factorise before you start solving.)

Q8 Rearrange into the form $x^2 + bx + c = 0$, then solve by factorising:

a) $x^2 - 2x = 15$
b) $x^2 + 5x = 14$
c) $x^2 + 6x = 16$
d) $x^2 + 4x = 21$
e) $x^2 + 5x = 36$

f) $x^2 + 4x = 45$
g) $x^2 - 3x = 10$
h) $x^2 = 5x$
i) $x^2 = 7x$
j) $x^2 = 11x$

k) $x^2 - 21 = 4x$
l) $x^2 - 63 = 2x$
m) $x^2 - 300 = 20x$
n) $x^2 + 48 = 26x$
o) $x^2 + 36 = 13x$

Q9 David is 3 years younger than his sister Jane.

a) If David is x years old, write down Jane's age as an expression containing x.

b) If the product of David and Jane's age is 130, use **a)** to form an equation involving x and then solve it.

c) How old is David?

Just in case you wondered... yes you do need to form a quadratic equation for Q9. Multiply out the expression from a), then treat it like Q8 — rearrange, factorise, solve. You'll have to pick the sensible answer though — there'll be one that doesn't make sense.

Questions on Recognising Graphs

Remember, you're going to need to be able to <u>sketch a graph</u> from <u>memory</u> — scary, huh. Don't worry — they don't expect you to remember them all (phew) but here are the ones you really need to know:

1) Straight line graph: $y = mx + c$

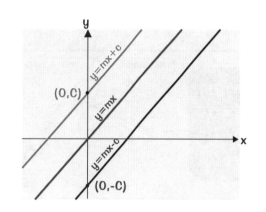

2) Reciprocal graphs: $y = a/x$

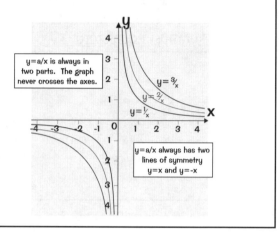

$y=a/x$ is always in two parts. The graph never crosses the axes.

$y=a/x$ always has two lines of symmetry $y=x$ and $y=-x$

3) Quadratic graphs: $y = ax^2$

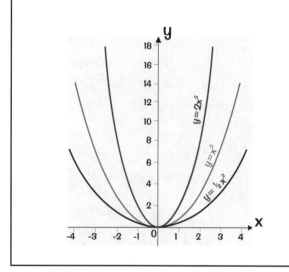

You can't find the <u>reciprocal of zero</u> because you can't <u>divide by zero</u>. So the reciprocal graph always has <u>two parts</u> — in diagonally opposite quadrants from each other — and neither touches the origin.

Q1 Sketch the graph of <u>$y = 4/x$</u> for values of x between -4 and 4, by first completing the table of values.

x	-4	-3	-2	-1	0	1	2	3	4
y			-2		✕			$1\frac{1}{3}$	

Q2 Sketch the following graphs:

a) $y = 5/x$

b) $y = x + 5$

c) $y = 5 - x$

d) $y = x^2 + 2$

e) $y = x^2 + 2x$

f) $y = x^2 + x + 1$

g) $y = 4x^2$

h) $y = 3x^2 - 1$

i) $y = 2x^2 + x - 6$

j) $y = 2x^2 + x$

k) $y = x + x^2$

l) $y = 7/x$

m) $y = 6x - 2$

n) $y = x - x^2$

o) $y = -x^2$

p) $y = -1/x$

Anyway, if you get stuck, you can always plot a graph using a table of values.

Questions on Circle Geometry

There's loads of vital things to know about circles —
so start practising and find out how much you know.

Q1 If AB is the <u>diameter</u> of the circle and O is
the centre, find the angles:

a) ADB

b) ABD

c) ADC

d) ACD

e) CBD

f) BAC

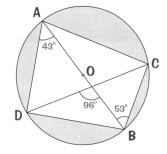

Q2 In each of the following parts
find the angle asked for and
say <u>why</u> this is the answer.

a) ∠ABC

b) ∠BCA

c) ∠BCT

d) ∠BDC

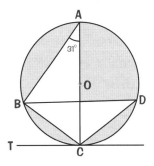

Make sure you remember your <u>triangle</u> stuff — you'll
need it for some of these. Especially the one about the
<u>interior</u> angles of a triangle <u>always</u> adding up to <u>180°</u>.

Q3 Find all the angles shown in the diagram. Give reasons for <u>at
least three</u> of the angles being what they are.

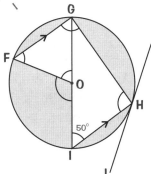

Q4 a) In <u>diagram A</u>, calculate the length CD.

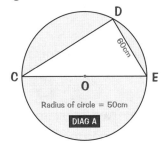

Radius of circle = 50cm

DIAG A

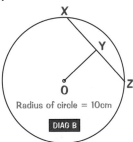

Radius of circle = 10cm

DIAG B

b) In <u>diagram B</u>, calculate the length OY if the chord is 16 cm long.

Q5 a) State the length BD in the diagram on the right.

b) Calculate the angle COD.

c) State the angle COB.

d) Find the angle CAB.

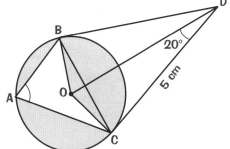

Questions on Similarity and Enlargement

You must remember the <u>important difference</u> between similarity and congruence.

Similarity and Congruence

1) Two shapes are <u>similar</u> if they're the <u>same shape</u> but different size. The lengths of the two shapes are related to the scale factor by this very important formula triangle:

2) Two shapes are <u>congruent</u> if they're the <u>same size</u> and <u>same shape</u>

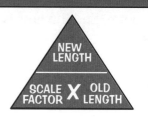

Q1 Two picture frames are shown. One picture is <u>similar</u> to the other. Calculate L cm, the length of the smaller frame.

Q2 For each of the following pairs:
a) Decide if the shapes are similar or not.
b) Give a reason for your answer.

i)

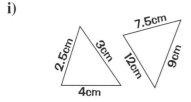

iii)

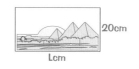

ii)

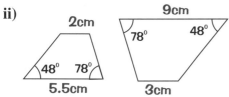

iv)

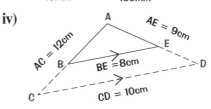

Q3 Angle ABC = Angle PQR and Angle BCA = Angle QRP
If triangle ABC is similar to triangle PQR, calculate the lengths of:

a) AB   b) QR

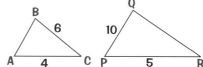

Q4 A rectangular picture is to be mounted on cardboard that leaves a border of 4 cm all the way around it. If the picture is 160 mm x 80 mm, are the two rectangles <u>similar</u>?

Q5 Which of these must be <u>similar</u> to each other?
a) Two circles   c) Two rectangles   e) Two equilateral triangles
b) Two rhombuses   d) Two squares   f) Two isosceles triangles

Q6 a) Express the ratio 64 cm : 5 m in the form 1 : x, giving x correct <u>to 2 sf</u>.
b) Express the ratio 12 mm : 6 m in the form 1 : x.
c) Express the ratio 12 kg : 40 g in the form x : 1.

Q7 A baker wants to make a circular cake. She knows a recipe, which gives quantities of ingredients for baking in a cake tin 20 cm in diameter. Her cake tin is 28 cm in diameter. By which of the following scale factors will the circumference of the cake (the distance around the outside) be increased?

a) 1.4   b) 2   c) 2.8   d) 3   e) 4

Questions on Length, Area and Volume

Time to get your brain in gear

— these can get pretty confusing, believe me.

You need to know these three facts:

1) LENGTH FORMULAS always have LENGTHS OCCURING SINGLY
2) AREA FORMULAS always have lengths MULTIPLIED IN PAIRS
3) VOLUME FORMULAS always have lengths multiplied in GROUPS OF THREE

Q1 p, q and r are lengths. State for each of the following, whether the formula gives a <u>length</u>, an <u>area</u>, a <u>volume</u> or <u>none of these</u>:

a) $p + q$

b) $pq - rq$

c) $p^2q^2 + pr^2$

d) pr/q

e) $5pqr/10$

f) $\pi pqr/2$

g) $p^3 + q^3 + r^3$

h) $9pr^2 - 2q$

Q2 w, x, y and z are lengths. State for each of the following, whether the formula gives a <u>length</u>, an <u>area</u> or a <u>volume</u>, when numbers are substituted in for the dummy variables:

a) $\dfrac{xy}{w}$

b) $\dfrac{xy^2 - w^2y}{z^2}$

c) $\dfrac{x^3}{y} - 14wz$

d) $\dfrac{x^2}{w} + \dfrac{w^2}{y} + \dfrac{y^2}{z} + \dfrac{z^4}{x^3}$

Q3 a, b, and c are lengths, r is the radius, $\pi = 3.14$.
State whether the formula gives a <u>perimeter</u>, <u>area</u> or <u>neither</u> of these.

a) $3\pi r^2 + abc$

b) $6\pi r + a - 6c$

c) $17ab + \pi r^2$

d) $\dfrac{16abc}{8b}$

Q4 If r is a length, is $\frac{4}{3}\pi r^2$ a volume formula?

Q5 If b and h are lengths, is ½bh an area formula?

Q6 Is $\dfrac{h}{2}(x + y)$ an area formula, if x, y and h are lengths?

> **Remember :-**
> if r is a length,
> then r² is an area
> and r³ is a volume.

Q7 If x and h are lengths, could this be a perimeter formula?
$x + x + h + h + h$

Q8 Could ½Dd be a volume formula, given that D and d are lengths?

Q9 The following statements are <u>incomplete</u>. For each one, find out what is missing and rewrite the formula correctly:

a) Volume of a cube = l   (where l is the length)

b) Area of a circle = $\pi\frac{d}{2}$ (where d is the diameter)

c) Perimeter of a circle = πr (where r is the radius)

> If you ever see something like r⁶ (where r is a radius) then rub your eyes because it's gone wrong — unless you're an alien from a 6-dimensional universe, in which case you'll feel right at home.

Questions on Solids and Nets

Before you go any further — make sure you know these 4 facts...

Surface Area and Nets

1) SURFACE AREA only applies to solid 3-D objects. It's the TOTAL AREA of all the OUTER SURFACES added together.
2) There is no simple formula for surface area — you have to work out each side in turn and then ADD THEM ALL TOGETHER.
3) A NET is just A SOLID SHAPE folded out FLAT.
4) SURFACE AREA OF SOLID = AREA OF NET.

Q1 Match these three names with the 2-dimensional drawings of the 3-D shapes.

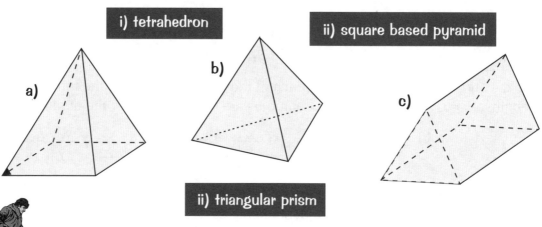

i) tetrahedron

ii) square based pyramid

a)

b)

c)

ii) triangular prism

There are 4 nets that you need to know inside out... so to speak:
1) Triangular Prism, 2) Cube, 3) Cuboid, 4) Pyramid. I reckon you
shouldn't read any further till you're 100% happy with them.

Q2 Draw an <u>accurate</u> 2-dimensional net that would fold to make the 3-D cuboid shown (diagram is not full size). It is not necessary to include flaps.

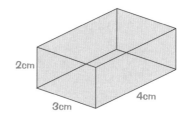

2cm
3cm
4cm

Q3 Draw a <u>full size net</u> (without flaps) of a square based pyramid whose base has sides of length 3 cm.

Q4 This unfinished isometric drawing shows a cuboid with dimensions 1 cm by 4 cm by 3 cm.

a) Complete the isometric drawing of the cuboid.

b) Draw the front elevation, side elevation and plan of the cuboid. Make sure your drawings are to scale.

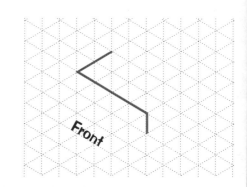

Front

STAGE THREE

Questions on Solids and Nets

If the question asks for flaps, remember you'll only need one on each join.

Q5 The net shown will fold to make a cube. Only one flap is shown. <u>Copy</u> the diagram.

a) Put an X in each corner that touches Y when the cube is made up.

b) Put an F where the flap will join one face to another, when the cube is made up.

c) Put on the other flaps necessary to glue the cube together.

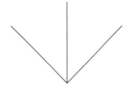

Q6 Using these <u>starting lines</u>, draw a cube.

Q7 a) What shape is the <u>base</u> of the cuboid shown opposite?

b) Which edges are the same length as DE?

c) Which lengths equal CE?

d) Which lengths equal the diagonal DG?

e) How many vertices has the cuboid?

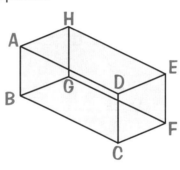

Q8 Draw a <u>circular cone</u>.

a) How many vertices does it have?

b) How many edges?

Q9 An equilateral triangular prism has a tetrahedron placed on top of it. For this <u>combined</u> solid,

a) How many edges does it have?

b) How many vertices?

c) How many faces?

Q10 A <u>regular hexagonal prism</u> has eight faces, two regular hexagons and six rectangles. Sketch the net of a regular hexagonal prism.

Q11 A net of a solid is shown opposite.

a) What is the name of the 3D solid?

b) How many vertices does it have?

c) Which other corners meet at D? Put an X at each one.

d) Draw a <u>3-D representation</u> of the solid this net represents.

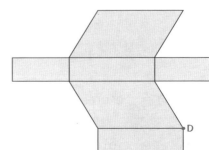

Q12 Draw <u>accurately</u> the net of a tetrahedron, with sufficient flaps to glue it together.

Questions on Vectors

The Four Notations — weren't they a... no, never mind. You've got to know all of these, so you can spot vectors a mile off and prepare yourself for the worst...

Q1 Write down the vectors lettered, then calculate the resultant vector. Check the resultant from the diagram.

e.g.

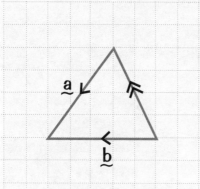

$$a = \begin{pmatrix} -3 \\ -4 \end{pmatrix} \qquad b = \begin{pmatrix} -5 \\ 0 \end{pmatrix}$$

$$-a + b = \begin{pmatrix} 3 \\ 4 \end{pmatrix} + \begin{pmatrix} -5 \\ 0 \end{pmatrix} = \begin{pmatrix} -2 \\ 4 \end{pmatrix}$$

as in the triangle.

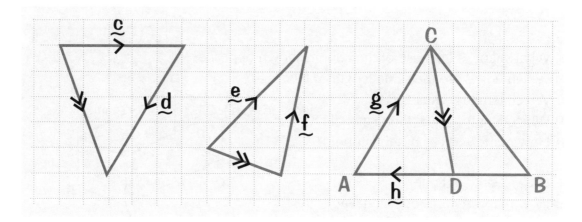

Q2 $p = \begin{pmatrix} 2 \\ 3 \end{pmatrix}$, $q = \begin{pmatrix} 0 \\ -2 \end{pmatrix}$, $r = \begin{pmatrix} 3 \\ -1 \end{pmatrix}$, $s = \begin{pmatrix} -1 \\ -2 \end{pmatrix}$

Calculate then draw:

a) $p + q$　　　　　**c)** $2r$　　　　　**e)** $2p - 2s$　　　　　**g)** $2r - q$　　　　　**i)** $p + 2s$
b) $p - q$　　　　　**d)** $s + p$　　　　　**f)** $3q + s$　　　　　**h)** $\tfrac{1}{2}q + 2r$　　　　**j)** $q - 2r$

Q3 M is the midpoint of WX
　　　$a = WZ$ and $b = WM$

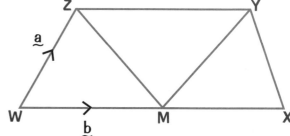

If MY = c, express in terms of a, b and c,

a) MZ　　　**b)** MX　　　**c)** ZX　　　**d)** XY　　　**e)** ZY　　　**f)** WY

STAGE THREE

Questions on Vectors

Q4   ABCDE is a pentagon.

$$\overrightarrow{AB} = \begin{pmatrix} 3 \\ 3 \end{pmatrix} \qquad \overrightarrow{AC} = \begin{pmatrix} 2 \\ 6 \end{pmatrix} \qquad \overrightarrow{AD} = \begin{pmatrix} -2 \\ 6 \end{pmatrix} \qquad \overrightarrow{AE} = \begin{pmatrix} -3 \\ 2 \end{pmatrix}$$

a) Draw this pentagon accurately.

b) Write down the vectors:

   i) $\overrightarrow{DE}$ **ii)** $\overrightarrow{DC}$ **iii)** $\overrightarrow{EC}$

c) What sort of triangle is $\triangle ACD$?

Q5

$$\overrightarrow{OX} = 3a + 3b$$
$$\overrightarrow{OY} = 5a + 2b$$
$$\overrightarrow{OZ} = 6a$$

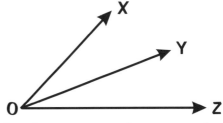

This diagram is not drawn to scale

Express in terms of a and b:

a) $\overrightarrow{XY}$ **c)** $\overrightarrow{XZ}$

b) $\overrightarrow{YZ}$ **d)** What 2 facts does this tell you about triangle OXZ?

Q6

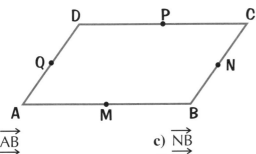

ABCD is a parallelogram.

MNPQ are mid points of the sides, as shown.

If $\overrightarrow{MQ} = \underset{\sim}{x}$ and $\overrightarrow{AM} = \underset{\sim}{y}$

Express in terms of $\underset{\sim}{x}$ and $\underset{\sim}{y}$:

a) $\overrightarrow{AB}$ **c)** $\overrightarrow{NB}$ **e)** $\overrightarrow{AC}$

b) $\overrightarrow{AQ}$ **d)** $\overrightarrow{BC}$ **f)** $\overrightarrow{BD}$

Q7   In the diagram on the right, EB and AC are perpendicular. ABCE is a parallelogram.
   $\angle EDC$ is a right angle.

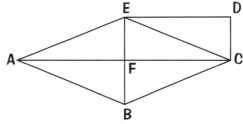

Name a vector equal to:

a) $\overrightarrow{FC}$ **c)** $\overrightarrow{BC}$ **e)** $2\overrightarrow{CD}$ **g)** $\overrightarrow{EF} - \overrightarrow{CF}$

b) $\overrightarrow{FB}$ **d)** $\overrightarrow{CE}$ **f)** $\overrightarrow{AE} + \overrightarrow{EC}$ **h)** $\overrightarrow{ED} + \overrightarrow{DC} + \overrightarrow{CB}$

If AC = 16 cm and EB = 6 cm
   i) What is the area of ABCE?
   ii) What is the area of ABCDE?

*Yep, you're gonna get to practise all
that right angled triangle stuff —
Pythagoras, Trig, that sort of thing.*

Oh, how the winter evenings will just fly by.

Questions on Real Life Vectors

Look at the pretty pictures... make sure you can see how this little lot fit with the questions.

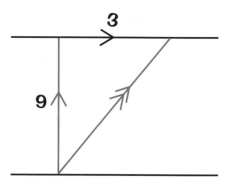

Q1 In still water my motor boat can achieve 9 km/hr. I aim the boat directly across the river which is running at 3 km/hr. What is my resultant velocity?

Q2

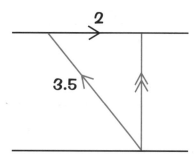

A girl wants to swim straight across a river running at 2 km/hr. If she can swim at 3.5 km/hr, calculate:

a) at what angle to the bank she should swim to go directly across

b) her resultant speed.

Q3 In the following diagrams the forces are acting on an object as shown.

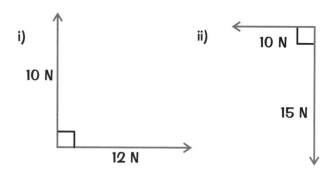

For each find:
a) the resultant force
b) its direction in relation to the larger force.

Q4 Two cranes are lifting a bridge girder into place. They exert forces of 65 kN and 75 kN at 24° and 21° to the vertical, respectively. What is the resultant upward force?

Q5 A Christmas tree is suspended in front of a building by two wires at 45° and 35° to the horizontal. If the tensions in the wires are equivalent to a force of 50 N vertically, find S and T.

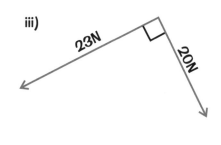

Q6 An aircraft is flying on a course of 290° at 350 km/hr. The wind is blowing and the aircraft actually flies on a bearing of 305° at 400 km/hr. Calculate the speed and direction of the wind.

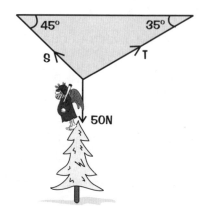

Questions on Loci and Constructions

Don't let a silly word like <u>locus</u> put you off — there are <u>easy</u> <u>marks</u> to be had here, but you've got to do everything neatly, using a pencil, ruler and compasses.

LOCUS — a line showing all points obeying the given rule.
CONSTRUCTIONS — accurate drawings using pencil, ruler and compasses, often to show a locus.

Q1 Two churches with bell towers are 3 km apart. On a still day, the sound of the bells can be heard 1.5 km away. Draw an accurate diagram to show the two churches and shade the area where <u>both</u> bells can be heard.

Q2 With the aid of a pair of compasses accurately draw an equilateral triangle with sides 5 cm. Now accurately draw a square with sides 6 cm.

Q3 **a)** Construct a triangle ABC in which AB is 6 cm, BC is 7.5 cm and AC is 5 cm long.
b) Construct the perpendicular bisector of AB and where this line meets BC, label the new point D.

Q4 On a beach children tend to buy ice creams from the nearest seller. On this diagram, construct a line to divide the children between the two ice cream sellers, so that each goes to the <u>nearest</u> one.

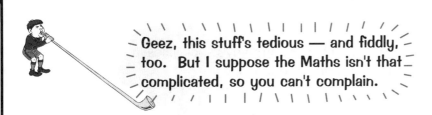

Geez, this stuff's tedious — and fiddly, too. But I suppose the Maths isn't that complicated, so you can't complain.

Q5 Tony likes to look at the tree in his garden. The diagram to the right shows the position of the tree relative to his bedroom window. Tony wants to postion his bed in such a way that he can see the tree in the morning as he awakes.

Carefully <u>shade</u> on the diagram the area in which Tony could position his bed.

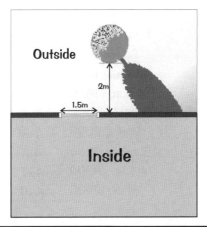

Questions on Time Series

Time Series — don't you just love 'em. These little horrors are pretty important, and could easily raise their ugly head in the Exam. Do yourself a favour and practise them.

Q1 Which of the following sets of measurements form time series?

a) The average rainfall in Cumbria, measured each day for a year.

b) The daily rainfall in European capital cities on Christmas Day, 2000.

c) The shoe size of everybody in Class 6C on September 1st, 2001.

d) My shoe size (measured every month) from when I was twelve months old to when I was fourteen years old.

Q2 a) Which two of the following time series are seasonal, and which two are not seasonal?

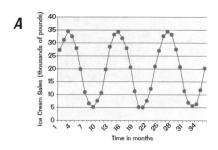
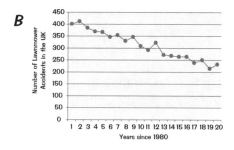
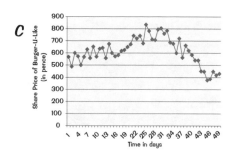
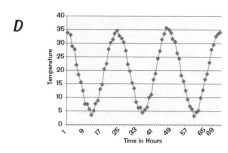

b) What are the periods of the time series which are seasonal?

c) Describe the trends in the time series which are **not** seasonal.

Q3 The following table shows the value of a knitwear company's sock sales in the years 1998-2000. The sales figures are given in thousands of pounds.

Time	Sales
Spring 1998	404
Summer 1998	401
Autumn 1998	411
Winter 1998	420
Spring 1999	416
Summer 1999	409
Autumn 1999	419
Winter 1999	424
Spring 2000	416
Summer 2000	413
Autumn 2000	427
Winter 2000	440

a) Plot the figures on a graph with time on the horizontal axis and sales on the vertical axis.

b) Calculate a 4-point moving average to smooth the series. Write your answers in the boxes provided.

c) Plot the moving average on the same axes as your original graph.

d) Describe the trend of the sales figures.

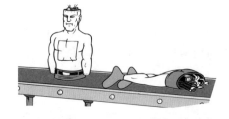

Questions on Tree Diagrams

A Likely Tree Diagram Question

I have a tub of sweets containing 4 lemon sherbets and 3 toffees. I take two sweets out to eat. Using a tree diagram, find the probability of both sweets being toffees.

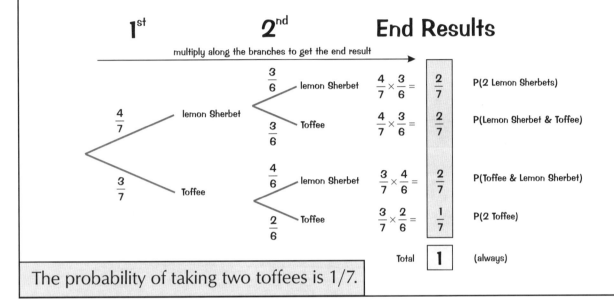

The probability of taking two toffees is 1/7.

Q1 Two marbles are taken from a box containing four red marbles, three green marbles and three white marbles. Draw a probability tree diagram to show this information. By using your tree diagram, find the probability that the two marbles taken from the box are the same colour.

Q2 An insurance company has 8 women and 14 men who are directors. From these directors a Chairperson and then a Personal Assistant are chosen at random by drawing names out of a hat. One person cannot be chosen for <u>both</u> positions.

a) What is the probability that a particular woman, Ruth, is chosen as the Chairperson?

b) Complete the tree diagram. Place in the brackets the probability associated with that particular stage.

c) An extra regulation is issued by the board of directors. This states that the Chairperson and Personal Assistant must be of opposite sexes. What are the chances of this happening without having to conduct the selection process a second time?

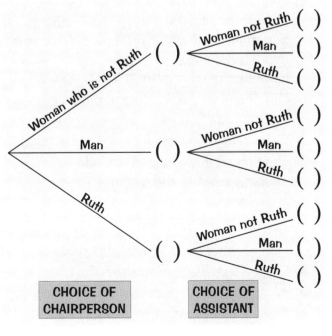

STAGE THREE

Questions on Tree Diagrams

If you have to draw a tree diagram yourself, just make sure you allow yourself plenty of room for all the possibilities.

Q3 A student needs to catch a <u>bus and a train</u> to get to university. The events and probabilities associated with each are shown on the tree diagram. For each event he can be <u>late</u> or <u>on time</u>. If he is <u>late</u> then he can catch the <u>next bus or train</u>. Work out the probability that:

a) the student <u>catches the bus</u> but <u>misses the train</u>

b) the student <u>misses the bus</u> but still manages to <u>catch the train</u>.

c) the student <u>misses</u> at least <u>one mode of transport</u> on his way to university.

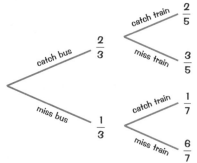

Q4 The probability that a football team will <u>win</u> a match is <u>50%</u>. By drawing a tree diagram, work out the chances of the team winning <u>four games in a row</u>.

Q5 The manager of the "Meat-Bar", a well-frequented burger franchise, has the sales figures in front of him for the last quarter. He sees in his sales column that they sold:

BURGERS	DRINKS
10,000 standard burgers	20,000 orange drinks
20,000 ginormous burgers	50,000 cola drinks
35,000 supreme burgers	30,000 weak lemon drinks
5,000 gut fillers	
	DESSERTS
FRIES	20,000 ice creams
60,000 portions of fries	10,000 doughnuts

a) The manager thinks that he can use the last quarter's sales figures to predict the probability of a customer buying a "<u>gut filler burger and a weak lemon drink, followed by a doughnut</u>". <u>How</u> do you think he does this? Write down your estimated probabilities in their <u>lowest terms</u>.

Ignoring the sales of fries, and by drawing a tree diagram or otherwise:

b) Discover the "meal" (<u>burger, drink and dessert</u>) that is <u>most likely</u> to be ordered, based on last quarter's figures.

c) What is the <u>probability</u> of that meal being sold?

d) How could the answer to **c)** help the manager operate the restaurant more effectively?

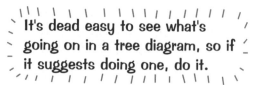

It's dead easy to see what's going on in a tree diagram, so if it suggests doing one, do it.

Q6 Two pool players, Sarah and Tina, play <u>3 games of pool</u> in a match. Sarah is not as good as Tina. <u>Sarah's</u> chance of <u>winning</u> a game is <u>45%</u>.

a) Draw a <u>tree diagram</u> to show the possible results of the 3 games.

b) What are the chances that <u>Tina</u> will win <u>all 3</u> games?

c) As long as 1 player <u>wins 2 or more</u> games then they will win the actual <u>match</u>. What are the chances that <u>Sarah will beat Tina</u> over the <u>3 game match</u>?